D0806394

WE ARE ONE

WE ARE ONE

40-DAY DEVOTIONAL JOURNEY

Walking by Faith
with the Persecuted Church

JOHNNIE MOORE

AUTHOR OF *THE MARTYR'S OATH*

TYNDALE
MOMENTUM™

The nonfiction imprint of
Tyndale House Publishers, Inc.

Visit Tyndale online at www.tyndale.com.

Visit Tyndale Momentum online at www.tyndalemomentum.com.

TYNDALE, *Tyndale Momentum*, and Tyndale's quill logo are registered trademarks of Tyndale House Publishers, Inc. The Tyndale Momentum logo is a trademark of Tyndale House Publishers, Inc. Tyndale Momentum is the nonfiction imprint of Tyndale House Publishers, Inc., Carol Stream, Illinois.

We Are One: Walking by Faith with the Persecuted Church

Designed by Mark Anthony Lane II

Published in association with Yates & Yates, LLP (www.yates2.com).

ISBN 978-1-4964-1950-7

Printed in China

24 23 22 21 20 19 18

7 6 5 4 3 2 1

CONTENTS

INTRODUCTION

WE ARE ONE

Holy Father, protect them by the power of your name, the name you gave me, so that they may be one as we are one.

JOHN 17:11

ON THE NIGHT before Jesus was crucified, he prayed for his disciples—not just for the ones who were with him in the Garden of Gethsemane but also for us today. What was on Jesus' heart when the Cross was in his sights was that all believers—in his time and in the future—"may be one."

We live in fractured times of political, cultural, and religious division, even among those who claim to follow Christ. But Jesus' prayer for us is a reminder that deeper and stronger than the things that divide us is the bond we share. *We are one.*

It is amazing, then, that for many Christians in the West, we have forgotten a large part of the family of God. According to some estimates, a Christian is martyred for his or her faith every five minutes. Christians in Egypt have experienced more persecution in the last five years than in the previous six hundred years combined. Groups like ISIS and Boko Haram terrorize Christians in the Middle East and Africa, and atheistic regimes in China and North Korea have worked to sideline and silence Christians. And the West is largely silent.

How can this be when we are one?

The goal of this devotional is to remember our brothers and sisters around the world who are suffering and dying because of their love for Jesus. But more than remembering them, we need to pray for them. We need to serve them. We need to identify with them. We need to *be* them.

Jesus' prayer is that we may be one. That is my prayer as well as you read these stories of those who have faced persecution around the world. Each devotion includes a short prayer that will help you as you intercede on behalf of your brothers and sisters facing persecution.

These devotions are a good place to start in identifying with those who are persecuted, but there are many more resources available to you through organizations like Open Doors USA (www.opendoorsusa.org) or my own organization, The KAIROS Trust (www.theKAIROStrust.com). My book *The Martyr's Oath* also contains more information about persecution worldwide as well as what you can do to support persecuted Christians. I've included the introduction and first chapter of that book at the back of this devotional. (You can take your stand with Christians around the world in harm's way at www.MartyrsOath.com.)

The apostle Paul wrote, "There is one body and one Spirit, just as you were called to one hope when you were called; one Lord, one faith, one baptism; one God and Father of all, who is over all and through all and in all" (Ephesians 4:4-6). There is one Lord over all of us who claim the name of Christ. We *are* one. My prayer is that we will live this reality.

Johnnie Moore
August 2017

DAY 1

ENOUGH

Everyone who has left houses or brothers or sisters or father or mother or wife or children or fields for my sake will receive a hundred times as much and will inherit eternal life.

MATTHEW 19:29

PERSECUTED CHRISTIANS know what it's like to rely on God for their daily needs. Often they've had to learn this lesson when everything was taken from them quickly and unexpectedly. Even while I was writing this book, one Egyptian village was nearly destroyed. Eighty Christian homes were looted and burned to the ground.

All of this was for one reason, because of a *rumor* that the Christians intended to build a new church in the city. When jihadist fanatics attacked, the police largely stood on the sidelines. These families watched as all they had was taken away and their homes were burned to ashes.

Their kids' toys and family photos, their lives and livelihoods gone.

We all hope this is an experience we never have, but we must believe that God would be with us if it did happen. He will provide what we need and reward us for our sacrifice on his account.

Here's a fact you can count on: God will always take care of you. That doesn't mean that you'll always have what you want. It doesn't mean that your cupboards won't be empty and your bank account won't run dry. It's not a guarantee of an easy life.

It is a guarantee of provision. It is a guarantee of enough.

God will give you enough of what you need when you need it, and he will give you enough grace to get through when it's hard to see the way, though God often doesn't give you too much, because he wants you to walk by faith. He knows you're better off if you know you need him every day.

God, be with my brothers and sisters who will lose their homes and lives today for you. May their testimony bring you glory and bring countless people to you. God, be with me today as I struggle to walk by faith. I thank you that you are always here for me, in abundance and in poverty.

DAY 2

FAITH LIKE A CHILD

Jesus said, "Let the little children come to me, and do not hinder them, for the kingdom of heaven belongs to such as these."

MATTHEW 19:14

NO MATTER OUR AGE, when we first enter a relationship with Christ, we come as "little children." Perhaps like me, you can recall the innocent faith you had when you first received Christ. Often, as we grow in the intellectual knowledge of our beliefs, we lose that fresh faith. And yet, that childlike faith can be the strongest substance on earth—stronger even than ISIS.

In an attack a few years ago, ISIS militants captured four Iraqi children and threatened to kill them unless they converted. "No, we can't do that," the children said. The militants pressured and threatened them: "Say the words!"

The determined children looked right back at those

fierce, armed jihadists and said, "No, we love Yasua [Jesus]. We have always loved Yasua. We have always followed Yasua. Yasua has always been with us."

At that, the ISIS fighters beheaded all four children.

These martyred children did not face their tormentors with a rational argument based on theological knowledge. They faced death with courage, strength, bravery, and an unflinching faith in Christ—"childlike faith." Jesus taught us about childlike faith with these words: "Truly, I say to you, unless you turn and become like children, you will never enter the kingdom of heaven. Whoever humbles himself like this child is the greatest in the kingdom of heaven" (Matthew 18:2-4, ESV).

We face a world with constant challenges and trials, even if not all are matters of life and death. We can learn from these children of the persecuted church to face our fears, our worst challenges, with childlike faith.

Are you facing a crisis or challenge today? Think of these four brave children. Face your trials with boldness and with an unwavering faith in God. Our role is to run to Jesus, cling to Jesus, and "cast all [our] anxiety" (1 Peter 5:7) on Jesus. That's the childlike faith Jesus told us to have. You don't need "great" faith, just childlike faith.

God, please be with the persecuted children who are being threatened with their lives for your sake this very day. Give them great boldness to endure suffering and, when needed, to stand up to their tormentors. Let their testimony be a challenge to me not to be consumed with the challenges I'm facing today. Help me to have more childlike faith and to trust you with my whole heart in all the difficulties I face.

DAY 3

ON ALL THE TIME

To me, to live is Christ and to die is gain.

PHILIPPIANS 1:21

MANY PERSECUTED CHRISTIANS live literally as Paul wrote, "to live is Christ." They are not like Christians in free countries. They can never go out in public—to the store, to a friend's house, to walk the dog—without people knowing they are Christians. A single Christian might stand out unavoidably in an entirely Islamic or Hindu portion of the world. Christians can never ignore their faith at work, school, or home, because everyone knows who they are. Members of the persecuted church live on a very narrow road. For some, there is never a moment, waking or sleeping, without watchful eyes, without danger.

In October 2011, Father Adeyi, a Catholic priest in terror-plagued Nigeria, said, "In spite of the many challenges, priests will not give up but are determined to run the race of faith to the end." He was referencing the apostle Paul, who often spoke of the Christian life as running a race. Paul wrote, "I have fought the good fight, I have finished the race, I have kept the faith" (2 Timothy 4:7, ESV).

Father Adeyi did finish his course. On April 24, 2016, militants kidnapped him, then used Father Adeyi's own cell phone to call his parish and demand a ransom. The parish raised almost ten thousand dollars, but the priest was not released. Two months later, the priest's decaying body was found dumped in a park.

For us, "to live is Christ" might be just a song lyric or a verse of Scripture we've memorized, but for the persecuted church, that phrase really does mean that Christ is everything to them. It means "it is no longer I who live, but Christ who lives in me" (Galatians 2:20, ESV). It means that every waking minute, they are cognizant of their faith, thinking of Christ, living for Christ, willing to die for Christ. When you think about it, "to live is Christ" is really the only way to actually live out the Christian life.

Unlike members of the persecuted church, every day

we face a world that offers many choices. We can make decisions without a thought about our Christian life, or we can make decisions as Christ directs us. Freedom is a wonderful blessing, but we cannot allow our freedom to give us the liberty to turn our Christianity on or off. All Christians owe it to Christ to be "on" all the time.

Remember our persecuted brothers and sisters as you make your decisions today. Be "all in" with your Christianity. Make it a goal to start each day saying, as Paul did, "To live is Christ."

God, please forgive me for making choices without depending on you. And please be with my brothers and sisters today who don't have such freedom to choose. Help those whose every move could bring on torture or even death. Help me depend on you every day, each step, each decision, so I also can truly say, along with the persecuted church, "To live is Christ."

DAY 4

GRACE FOR DENIERS AND DOUBTERS

I tell you, my friends, do not be afraid of those who kill the body and after that can do no more. But I will show you whom you should fear: Fear him who, after your body has been killed, has authority to throw you into hell. Yes, I tell you, fear him.

LUKE 12:4-5

A PERSECUTED FATHER in Iraq faced an impossible decision when he was confronted by armed militants. They didn't threaten to torture or kill him. Instead, they threatened to murder his children. He would have to watch them die one by one unless he told the gunmen he would follow Muhammad.

Jesus told us not to fear those who can kill the body. So, what was the right decision? Would this father be failing as a Christian if he didn't sacrifice his children for a statement to follow Christ? Or would he be failing as a Christian father if he succumbed to his fear and allowed these intruders to murder his children, fearing man over God?

This father faced the fact that his children were about to be brutally murdered in front of his eyes, and he would have to live with that. He looked at his attackers, then looked at his children, and repeated the words to follow Muhammad. When the attackers left, he quickly called his priest and repented, saying, "I have always loved Yasua [Jesus]. I said those words because I couldn't see my children be killed."

We cannot stand in that father's place and choose for him, one way or the other. But we can sit in the safety of our homes and appreciate this: out of all the decisions this father made for his children, he made the decision to raise his children to know Christ in the first place, even though it meant it might cost his own life or theirs. If this man had not identified himself with Christ and his church from the beginning, if he and his children had not been known as Christians all around town, he would never have had to face those attackers at all.

Thankfully, God's grace extends even to denial and doubt. Like the apostle Thomas, who doubted Jesus had been resurrected, and the apostle Peter, who denied being a friend of Jesus, the Iraqi father found forgiveness. In the end, Peter died for Jesus' name, and Thomas was the only apostle mentioned in the Bible who touched the wounds of Jesus. They moved beyond their moments of weakness with the most intimate experiences of Jesus' grace.

In the aftermath of that father's choice—a choice some would say was weakness and others would say was heroic—God was always there, offering grace. Just as he extends grace to us in our moments of denial, doubt, discouragement, and distrust. And just as grace would be available even to the terrorists who murder Christians should they themselves come to repentance.

Perhaps you have experienced a difficult or painful choice; perhaps you've doubted Jesus or even denied him. Here's what you can count on: God's grace. It is fully available to you in moments of strength and in your moment of greatest weakness.

God, I thank you for your grace toward your followers around the world. Please flood with your Spirit those who are struggling to stand up for you under serious threats. Your merciful, powerful, and forgiving grace covers their weakness, even as I pray you make them strong. I thank you that your grace is not weaker but stronger in my doubts and denial. You are with me when I am at my weakest. Your power is strongest when I'm the most powerless. I praise you that I cannot run beyond the reach of your mercy.

DAY 5

EXPECT PERSECUTION

Blessed are you when people hate you, when they exclude you and insult you and reject your name as evil, because of the Son of Man.

LUKE 6:22

IN PAKISTAN IN 2016, a man complained to the police that the music coming from a nearby church was too loud. As a result, officers stormed the church during the service and beat up the pastor in front of his congregation. It was a terrible ordeal—terrible for the pastor and terrible for his family and congregation members who had to stand by, unable to help. It was terrible, yet not unusual. Pakistan normally ranks within the top ten of worst countries for Christians, yet it has millions of them.

With such an awful intrusion even being possible, it can seem amazing to Christians in the free world that persecuted Christians keep going to church at all. We make decisions not to attend church because the air conditioning is too cold, the parking lot is too crowded, or the music is too loud.

Perhaps the problem isn't inconvenience but expectations. We expect the church to cater to our needs. We expect church to be comfortable, convenient, and cozy. We want good customer service and pleasantries. Yet, Jesus' expectation for the church was far less domesticated.

Jesus taught us to *expect* persecution for being a part of the church—to expect danger, disruption, and disorder! He encouraged all followers by saying, "Blessed are you when others revile you and persecute you and utter all kinds of evil against you falsely on my account. Rejoice and be glad, for your reward is great in heaven" (Matthew 5:11-12, ESV). Stop and think about this. So much for catering to my desire for convenience!

Could it be that in the free church we ought to experience more persecution? We don't deal with much of it, not only because we live in a country that allows religious freedom but also because it's easy to coast by as undercover Christians. It's easy to simply avoid controversy, criticism, and conflict by not speaking up. If we don't give voice to our faith, no one will know of our commitment, and no one will bother us.

Here's a thought: our desire for convenience and comfort even in church might be an indication of our passion to welcome outsiders in, but it might also be key evidence of our self-centeredness. We're not making the place comfortable for those seeking Christ but for those of us who've already found him.

Father, I pray for pastors in all the persecuted countries of the world, that you would bless them in their trials. Give them courage to keep standing up for you and leading people toward you. And God, please give me courage to do the same. Help me to speak up for you to others and to never forget that Christians all over the world are suffering for doing just that. Help me not to seek convenience ahead of your plan for my life and for the church.

DAY 6

A FAITH-DIVIDED FAMILY

I have come to set a man against his father, and a daughter against her mother, and a daughter-in-law against her mother-in-law. And a person's enemies will be those of his own household.

MATTHEW 10:35-36, ESV

AMIR AND ELISA are a Christian couple living in Lebanon. They both came from Muslim families in Egypt. When Elisa announced that she had converted to Christianity, her family threatened her. The persecution in her home became so severe that she fled to Beirut just to find a safe place to live.

In Beirut, she met Amir, a seminary student who was also from Egypt. They were married in a Christian ceremony. But in a persecuting country, nothing is simple. As Egyptian citizens, and because they are Christians, their marriage was not government sanctioned. Humiliated yet determined, Amir and Elisa pressed on, working through each difficulty with great confidence in the Lord. Today, both are pursuing degrees in higher education so they can work full-time in Christian ministry to share Jesus with their people.

Sometimes what stings the most is when people you expect to love you no matter what are the ones who turn on you, as Elisa's family turned on her. This is the experience of so many of our persecuted brothers and sisters around the world. As David wrote, "Even my close friend, someone I trusted, one who shared my bread, has turned against me" (Psalm 41:9).

Yet it is in our refusal to compromise, our willingness to make choices that set us apart, that we become more like Christ. Jesus said, "Everyone who has left houses or brothers or sisters or father or mother or wife or children or fields for my sake will receive a hundred times as much and will inherit eternal life" (Matthew 19:29). These choices, though, don't remove the hurt of a lost love for forbidden faith.

When the people closest to you let you down, turn against you, or betray you, Scripture promises that although you may have lost a family member, "there is a friend who sticks closer than a brother" (Proverbs 18:24). Jesus is your lifelong friend and your closest confidant. He loves you always. If you're fortunate to have the blessing of your family's support in your faith, that's a blessing you should never take for granted. Praise Jesus for it. And if you're ever fortunate to meet someone who doesn't have that blessing, then choose to be like family to that person.

God, help those whose families have rejected them for following you. Support them with your love, and guide them to those who will be like family to them. I pray also for family members who do not believe; I ask you to bring them to faith and to use the testimony of their believing family to draw them closer to you today.

DAY 7

FREED FROM SELF-IMPOSED PRISONS

Continue to remember those in prison as if you were together with them in prison, and those who are mistreated as if you yourselves were suffering.

HEBREWS 13:3

CHRISTIANS in the persecuted church often face stiff prison sentences simply because of their faith. The prison experience generally involves deprivation and torture.

Ladan is a beautiful young woman from Iran who was invited to a house church and became a believer in Christ. When her family saw the change in her and discovered her new faith, she knew her days were numbered. To escape being imprisoned, Ladan fled to Turkey.

As she matured in Christ, Ladan experienced a growing desire to return to Iran to share the gospel. Upon her return, Ladan handed out Christian literature and Bibles.

She saw many people become believers before she was eventually caught. Ladan was imprisoned and endured a lengthy interrogation but would not give the names of her fellow believers.

Eventually, she was sent to solitary confinement for twenty-five days, but she managed to smuggle a pen into her cell. With the help of the Holy Spirit, she recalled verses of Scripture. Day after day, she wrote them out on the cell walls.

After her imprisonment, Ladan was forced to leave Iran and her Muslim family for good. She remains deeply concerned about getting God's Word into her home country. Her prayer is that one day in heaven she will meet someone who became a Christian because of the words she left behind on the prison walls. I believe she will have that very experience.

In the West, we are not imprisoned for our faith, but many other influences can restrain us from sharing it. There is a prison of shame, a prison of bitterness, prisons of self-doubt, guilt, and unforgiveness. In these ways, we imprison ourselves, and we become our own persecutors. As a result, our life-giving faith doesn't show itself fully to those around us.

Perhaps you have something in your heart that keeps you from being a witness for Christ. God wants to take our self-imposed prisons and use them as testimonies of our faith for others. He wants us to break free. What an insult it would be to choose to imprison our faith when so many of our brothers and sisters around the world have imprisonment chosen for them.

Today is a good day to thank God for the physical freedom he has given you, but it is also a great day to break out of your self-imposed prisons, to let your light shine for him. Scribble God's Word on those dark places of your heart, and later someone else will find the power of Jesus through your freedom.

God, so many of our brothers and sisters are in prisons all over the world today because of their love for you. Please ease their suffering today, stop their tormentors, give them a voice for you inside their cells, and then free them from those cells. Reveal to me what might be imprisoning my own heart, and help me to break free as well. Please give me a burden and the boldness to share the Good News of Jesus with others, with the courage I see in the persecuted church.

DAY 8

WE ARE OVERCOMERS

Now who is there to harm you if you are zealous for what is good? But even if you should suffer for righteousness' sake, you will be blessed. Have no fear of them, nor be troubled.

1 PETER 3:13-14, ESV

CHRISTIAN MISSIONARIES enjoyed a long period of evangelism in China—from the famed J. Hudson Taylor and his China Inland Mission, to the stream of heroic Southern Baptist missionaries, many of whom were women, such as the legendary Lottie Moon. But preaching the gospel changed in a day, with the stroke of a pen. In 1949, the Chinese government began expelling every foreign Christian missionary. In 1959, the government expelled the last western Christian leader, Helen Willis, who with her husband, Christopher, ran the Christian Book Room that printed and distributed hymnals and portions of the Gospels.

Although churches were officially closed, by 1962, after only a few years of spiritual darkness, reports started trickling out to the West about the great strength of the Christian faith in China. Tiny "churches" of just a few courageous believers were often meeting together to share the Word and pray. By the time all religion was banned from China completely, during the Cultural Revolution in 1966, Christianity had a firm hold in small groups that dotted the vast nation.

How could a few groups of believers hold out, when they were scattered across a vast land inhabited by nearly a billion people who were indoctrinated in an anti-God philosophy? The government conspired against them, villagers persecuted them, neighbors spied on them, and police overpowered them. It would seem only a matter of time before Christianity would die out completely.

But God would not be locked out of China despite the Communist government's best efforts. Instead, faithful Christians managed to accomplish the impossible. In a word, they *won*. With this exponential rate of growth in the Chinese church, missiologists project that within the next fifteen years there will be more than two hundred million Christians in China.

Tertullian, an ancient church father, said, "The blood of the martyrs is the seed of the church." No power on earth is stronger than the name of Jesus Christ; no dominion can overtake the dominance of God's grace; no force compares to the strength of the Holy Spirit moving through the lives of believers.

And for you today, no matter what you may face, nothing can stop the work of God in and through your life as you yield to him. Paul, who was persecuted throughout his entire Christian life, wrote this: "We now have this light shining in our hearts, but we ourselves are like fragile clay jars containing this great treasure. This makes it clear that our great power is from God, not from ourselves" (2 Corinthians 4:7, NLT). God's power is total. His Word is absolute. In Christ, we have complete victory.

This is the story of the Chinese church, and it will be the story of our lives. We are overcomers. We are more than overcomers, for we have in Jesus' resurrection the death of death.

Father, the testimony of what happened in China helps me remember how great your power is to do the impossible. Real power comes from you. Please help me yield to you and depend on you more completely. And please, Lord, help those in persecuted countries be encouraged that they, too, can overcome because you have already won the victory for us.

DAY 9

RENEWED STRENGTH THROUGH SERVING

Let us not become weary in doing good, for at the proper time we will reap a harvest if we do not give up.

GALATIANS 6:9

IN IRAN just a few years ago, a thirteen-year-old girl said good-bye to her father as he left their house. After a while, she prepared tea for him, as he had requested, then waited for him to come home. He never came. Instead, family friends came with the news that he had been hanged for evangelizing.

The family was grief stricken. The daughter didn't know what to do without her father. She was worn out from the continued and ultimate persecution the family had experienced, and she was ready to give up. Then she decided to do something drastic: she would carry on his work. At age thirteen, she and some friends wrote out verses of Scripture on pieces of paper and left them lying around the town for people to find.

Next, she decided to write out the entire Gospel of John and leave it sitting out in an area where she felt the Lord direct her. Soon after this, she met some people who were translating and printing Bibles for Iran. She became involved with their task, and in less than three years, through their joint efforts, one million New Testaments were put into the hands of Iranians. When this girl was exhausted from grief and ready to give up, she listened for God's direction and followed his next step for her to accomplish his greater purposes.

God knows that his people get depleted by life. A tired apostle Paul wrote, "We were burdened beyond measure, above strength, so that we despaired even of life" (2 Corinthians 1:8, NKJV). God also knows how to restore us. After Paul rested, he wrote, "Let us not become weary in doing good" (Galatians 6:9).

Even Jesus grew weary, but he showed us one way to regain our strength. John recorded: "Jesus, worn out by the trip, sat down at the well" (John 4:6, MSG). As Jesus rested, he found a woman to minister to, and it rejuvenated him. After he rested, he said, "I have food to eat that you do not know about. . . . My food is to do the will of him who sent me and to accomplish his work" (John 4:32, 34, ESV). By doing the next thing God asks of us for someone else, we can find new energy.

By ministering to others, this young girl found the strength to carry on, and in her teens she reached more people than most people can reach in a lifetime of ministry. People get tired. Christians get tired. Yet, God tells us to "not become weary in doing good." The apostle Paul once wrote, "For this I toil, struggling with all *his* energy that he powerfully works within me" (Colossians 1:29, ESV, emphasis added).

In war and in sports, people find they can dig deeper to keep going. In Christianity, we dig deeper by doing God's work, in his strength. If you are tired, worn out from life or even from grief, the encouragement is to keep doing what you know to be right. One day, you'll also "reap a harvest." You might just change the world.

Lord, thank you for the heroes of faith operating around the world today, like this girl who rose above her circumstances to get your Word into Iran. I pray for all those who are translating, printing, and distributing Bibles into persecuted areas around the globe. Please help me remember their struggles even as I work to surmount my own. Keep me mindful not to become weary in doing good. I thank you for the promise that I will reap a harvest.

DAY 10

THE BEAUTIFUL CROSS

The message of the cross is foolish to those who are headed for destruction! But we who are being saved know it is the very power of God.

1 CORINTHIANS 1:18, NLT

SUSANNA'S HUSBAND had a cross tattooed on his arm. It was meant to be a public symbol of his private faith. He wasn't ashamed of his Christianity. He wasn't fearful of what others might think of it.

In fact, his courage extended far beyond that image on his wrist. He'd frequently talk of his faith to his Muslim friends in his country, which is almost entirely Islamic. But in the spring of 2017, Islamic terrorists got ahold of him.

They tried to force him to convert to Islam.

He refused. Instead, he pointed to the cross tattooed on his arm and said fearlessly, "I am a Christian!"

They responded by shooting him once in the head, and then they shot the cross in his wrist more than a dozen times. "Like the devil," Susanna said, "[the terrorists] get nervous when they see the cross."

When we see the cross, we sometimes don't feel anything at all. Her comment reminds me of James 2:19, where James writes sarcastically, "You believe that there is one God. Good! Even the demons believe that—and shudder."

James was saying that the demons often have more fear and respect for God than the children of God do!

The cross isn't an identifying symbol for many of us. It sits lonely atop churches and hangs unnoticed around our necks, and our association with the cross normally costs us nothing. This isn't the case with Christians throughout the persecuted world. They wear the cross as a symbol to the world that they aren't ashamed. The cross is a reminder of their own commitment to Jesus Christ, and wearing that cross could cost them their lives.

"The blood of the martyrs has already covered our whole city," Susanna said.

Now that group of Jesus' servants includes her husband of thirty years, the father of their three children. Yet she remains unashamed and is proud of the cross she has tattooed on her own wrist. She shared her husband's story with total faith and gratitude to God.

Having spent many years meeting with members of the persecuted church, I've seen with new eyes the power of the cross, the offense it is to those who do not believe, and the hope it is to those of us who do. I haven't tattooed it on my arm yet, but I carry a small cross around in my pocket almost every day and to almost every place. It is a reminder to me of the sacrifice of those who have died for Jesus. Maybe you'd like to do the same, but even if you don't, please don't miss the significance of the cross.

Father, the Cross cost you so much, and we value it so little. Please show us again its power in our own lives, and make it a testimony through us to the entire world. Give special grace to those today who have chosen not to hide their faith in the face of grave hostility. May their testimony be a brilliant light to all those who do not believe.

DAY 11

FAITH FOR ANOTHER WORLD

Pray for those who mistreat you.

LUKE 6:28

"**WHEN HE DIED,**" the woman said, "he was praying for those who did this to him."

The woman's brother was one of the victims of the terrible Palm Sunday attacks in Egypt in 2017. He was sitting in a pew when the bomb went off near him, nearly severing his leg and breaking other bones.

Unlike those sitting not far from him, he didn't die immediately. He later died in the hospital. His name, Fadi, is a common name among Egyptian Christians, and it means "redeemer." He was only twenty-two, and he was in his last year of college. He was studying the sciences, and in his free time he was very involved in the church. Fadi lived for Jesus during his life, and he was a testimony to him in his death—even praying for those who killed him with his dying breaths.

The strength of his faith left a lasting impression on those who loved him most. I met his family only two weeks after the tragedy, and his sister told me, "I believe that Fadi is in a great place, so that's why I'm happy."

Happy. What a word to choose within the context of such terrible tragedy!

Hearing her say that word within this story stopped me dead in my tracks. It revealed a strength of our faith that I've rarely seen in my own life or anywhere in the world. Fadi's family really, truly believed the Bible. They trusted Jesus with their tragedy, and they believed that Fadi was in a better place.

I think his dying prayer had everything to do with this. He spoke with the ethics of another world—forgiving his enemies—as he transitioned to that world himself. He didn't die angry or in doubt. He died with faith and forgiveness, and that faith inspired his family to carry on.

In Egyptian culture, as in our own, people customarily wear black when in mourning. Not Fadi's sister. She has decided to wear white, because she aims to wear "a garment of praise instead of a spirit of despair" (Isaiah 61:3).

†

God, when I read stories like Fadi's, they sometimes feel so far from where my heart is today. Please change me and give me faith that will be a supernatural light to all those around me. Help me to shine, and especially show me the way when life seems as dark as night. And please be with the believers around the world who will suffer. Please give them the peace and strength that you've given to Fadi's sister. You are a great and good God.

DAY 12

GOD'S PRESENCE IN OUR PAIN

Rejoice with those who rejoice; mourn with those who mourn.

ROMANS 12:15

GETTING CLOSE to the persecuted church helps put our own pain and problems in perspective. It also deepens our passion to pray for the persecuted church. We feel differently about our own difficulties, and we feel more deeply for theirs.

Take, for instance, the Syrian pastor, Mishail. He knows what it's like to "mourn with those who mourn" as much as anyone in the world, as he literally had to fulfill his ministry in the line of fire.

In the heart of the Syrian conflict, he told a reporter that death and destruction at the hands of ISIS were so pervasive that he once witnessed body parts flying through the air. He didn't talk about an isolated incident but about one of many such incidents. The people's previously peaceful lives had collapsed into chaos. He was living every day in an unbearable horror movie.

What broke his heart the most were the parents grieving the deaths of their sons and daughters. Maybe you know that pain all too well. The pain of losing a child is said to be the worst in the world. You love your children entirely, and you walk with them through every phase of life. In a real sense, they *are* your life, and when they lose their lives, it's as if you've lost part of your own.

In one incident alone, Pastor Mishail recounts burying twenty young men, teenagers and twentysomethings. They were all sons of grieving mothers and fathers.

Sometimes, he told the reporter, they didn't even have the bodies to bury: "We have performed burial prayers over many shirts of the ones whose bodies were not found."

The grieving parents, Mishail said, would bring their children's best clothes, often a wedding suit or a shirt with a tie and jeans. The spiritual leaders would pray over the clothes as they buried them, doing the funeral without the body.

These parents knew firsthand what the psalmist calls being "crushed in spirit." Their hearts didn't just break; they were crushed. Yet, we worship a Lord who is "close to the brokenhearted" (Psalm 34:18) and who doesn't hide his face from our cries for help.

I've seen in the eyes of so many persecuted believers a different type of intimacy in their relationships with Jesus. They know him as a friend who has walked with them in their pain and fear, not simply as a god whom they worship. I hope you never have to endure the kind of pain these men and women have endured, but because of their stories, I know Jesus will be with you, too.

Whatever happens—however crushed you might feel—he is there. Know that even when you cry out to the sky, "Why?" you simultaneously acknowledge your belief that he is the answer—for in your questioning of him, you are showing you still have faith in him.

Dear God, I thank you that there is no crushed heart that has to be alone. Be with our suffering brothers and sisters whose pain is beyond words and whose hope is only in you. In my moments of heartbreak may I find you close to me. In my moments of peace may I find another path to intimacy with you. I thank you that you are with me when circumstances are good and when they are not.

DAY 13

BLESSED BY INSULT

If you are insulted for the name of Christ, you are blessed, because the Spirit of glory and of God rests upon you. . . . Yet if anyone suffers as a Christian, let him not be ashamed, but let him glorify God in that name.

1 PETER 4:14, 16, ESV

IT'S AN OFTEN overlooked part of the Christmas story: after the angels, shepherds, and wise men came, Joseph and Mary fled to Egypt to find a sanctuary for young Jesus under the constant threats of King Herod. The Egyptian church has long celebrated this moment as its founding.

For centuries, Christianity flourished in Egypt after the Christ child lived there, and to this day there are still at least ten million Christians in the predominantly Islamic country. But in the last few years, the Christian population in Egypt has been under near-constant attack from jihadists. Some estimate that the church has experienced more persecution in the last five years than in the previous six hundred years combined.

It's particularly hard for children in some places. Instead of being a sanctuary, Egypt is often a nation of anxiety and fear for them. Christian children are sometimes singled out in their classes, bullied by "friends," and indoctrinated by authority figures who tell them that the Christian God is not the right god and that the Bible is corrupt. Even so young, they are "insulted for the name of Christ." Children act like children all over the world, and in Egypt they're still just children. Some lash out or innocently try to convince their friends of the validity of their faith.

Then there are the more severe cases where some Christian children in Egypt have been arrested and held for as long as three years just because their innocent remarks were interpreted as speaking against Islam. While the government of the country officially tolerates the Christian community, there are parts of the country where Christians are severely treated either by local rogue authorities or by extremists embedded in the culture. According to these radicals, even children must submit.

Peter told us it is our glory to be insulted because of our faith, for it proves to us that we have clearly demonstrated our faith to the world. Others would not insult us if they didn't know of our love for Jesus. Christian parents in the persecuted church around the world must prepare their children for the inevitable insults, and sometimes worse.

The brave believers, though they live in what one minister calls a "culture of fear," have a deeper faith than many of us, despite our access to unlimited Bible resources and religious freedom. We become enraged if we are insulted for our faith, and we demand our rights. They simply receive their insults and thank God that their light was shining brightly enough to even be noticed.

Maybe we ought to be insulted more often for Jesus.

God, please help persecuted parents train their children to be wise in their expressions of faith, resilient in their beliefs, and bold in letting their light shine for Christ, regardless of the cost. And I ask the same for myself today. Help me, Lord, to become wiser and more open in my expressions of faith, deeper in my beliefs, and bolder in letting my light shine for you, regardless of what people might do to me or say about me. Please help me do my part to prepare the next generation to stand strong for you too. In the name of Jesus, I pray.

DAY 14

A WISE INVESTMENT

I know you are enduring patiently and bearing up for my name's sake, and you have not grown weary.

REVELATION 2:3, ESV

FOR MORE THAN sixty years China has been responsible for some of the worst persecution in the history of Christendom. But China also is a place of flourishing Christianity.

Thousands of Chinese people come to Christ every day. With a total Chinese population of nearly a billion and a half people, there will eventually be more Christians in China than there are in the United States, if the church hasn't already, quietly, grown to this size. How could this be?

In the thirty years of severe persecution that came after China began expelling all foreign missionaries in 1949, Christianity at first declined but then began to explode. Great heroes of the faith were rounded up, such as Pastor

Samuel Lamb, who was imprisoned and sentenced to slave labor in the coal mines. For two decades, along with many other Christian prisoners, Pastor Lamb prayed for the disciples he had been forced to leave. In desperate conditions as an inmate, Pastor Lamb personified the scriptural virtues of enduring patiently, bearing up for Christ's sake, and not growing weary.

World politics began to shift and brought the release of some Christians from prison. Pastor Lamb was finally able to return to his home after twenty years, only to discover that the tiny flock he left behind had grown into a huge body of thousands of believers. I visited Pastor Lamb late in his life. After having Communion with hundreds of his congregants in one of his dozens of services, I sat with him in an upper room of the house where they were meeting. He recounted to me his testimony of how his church exploded while he was in prison and concluded with a few simple words that I've never forgotten: "Persecution is good."

Can you imagine the joy Pastor Lamb felt to discover his tremendous sacrifice and steadfast faith were not in vain? The same will be true for you. When you go through a season of unjust suffering, that season is not one of loss but of investing in the future. It's a season of blessing, not a curse. It's a season of hope, not helplessness. It's a season fully within the control of God's will, for his purposes, seated squarely in his plan.

Regardless of the load you may be bearing today, remember your Chinese brothers and sisters. Remember Pastor Samuel Lamb. If you hold fast to your faith without growing weary, you also will be surprised at what the Lord can do with this time of discomfort, pain, and trial. For as the apostle Paul wrote, "In all things God works for the good of those who love him, who have been called according to his purpose" (Romans 8:28).

Father, you know that life sometimes is not easy, and yet reading about what these Chinese Christians have endured makes me want to break out in praise to you. Thank you for the testimony of the persecuted church. Please be with those Christians who are patiently enduring in prison cells for the sake of the gospel. Please help me to endure more patiently, to bear up, and to not grow weary as I press on in life with you. Thank you, Lord.

DAY 15

TO THOSE WHO KILL US

I say to you, love your enemies . . . and pray for those who . . . persecute you. . . . For if you love those who love you, what reward have you? Do not even the tax collectors do the same?

MATTHEW 5:44, 46, NKJV

BOMBS BLEW UP at two historic Coptic churches in Egypt on Palm Sunday 2017, killing nearly fifty parishioners and injuring more than one hundred others.

Just hours after the blast, amid outrage and grief, Father Boules George stepped before his packed church and gave the terrorists a three-point sermon that went viral worldwide. It was entitled "A Message to Those Who Kill Us." His three points were simple but not cliché: "Thank you," "We love you," and "We're praying for you."

Father George said "Thank you" because the terrorists gave the dead the honor to die as Christ died; because the terrorists shortened the victims' journey to their heavenly home; because the terrorists allowed Christians to fulfill Christ's words in Luke 10:3 (NKJV), "Behold, I send you out as lambs among wolves"; and because the terrorists' actions made people mindful of their eternal destinies. The church was, in fact, now overflowing with people who didn't ordinarily attend.

Then Father George said "We love you" because even murderers and thieves love those who love them, but only followers of Jesus are taught to love our enemies. Father George closed his message with "We're praying for you" because, he reasoned, if a terrorist could taste the love of God even one time, it would drive hatred from his heart.

The love of Christ articulated by Father George and so common in the persecuted church is so rich, so pure, and so divine that it shocks the rest of the world. This forgiving love makes headlines. It stops even Christians in their tracks.

Yet if this unconditional love is at the heart of our faith, then why do we see it so rarely? God calls each of us to choose a path of love and forgiveness not simply in the face of severe persecution but in our everyday lives. Every time someone treats us offensively, we are to forgive and to love. Every time someone is unkind to us, we are to forgive and to love. Every chance we can, we forgive and we love.

Love is what Christians are called to *do*, because unconditional love is what Jesus offered to us!

We must learn to walk in love—perhaps slowly at first, but as we take steps toward growing in love toward others, we grow in love with God, because God *is* love. We walk in love toward the person who cheated us, who lied to us, who treated us unfairly. We walk in love, perhaps with baby steps, but we *walk*, nonetheless.

When we open ourselves to show the love of God in a way that costs something, we find the true supernatural power of our faith. Father George's words to those hate-filled terrorists were words of life to harbingers of death. The fact that he even could say them represents a parting of the Red Sea in his heart; every act of unconditional love is itself a miracle. It is an injection of heaven's values into a world in which we're totally content to love only those who love us.

If we love those who are against us, we display God's real love to a world that needs to see it.

Lord, I can only imagine how difficult it would be for persecuted Christians to respond with your love to their tormentors. Please fill them with your love for them today so that they will have the grace to show that love to those who attack them. It's hard to imagine loving those who despise me, when I struggle just to love those who casually dislike me. Today, help me to respond with grace, not wrath, and with peace, not out of pain. Today, I join my voice with the psalmist to say, "Your unfailing love is better than life itself; how I praise you!" (Psalm 63:3, NLT).

DAY 16

FIGHTING A SPIRITUAL BATTLE

Deliver me, O Lord, from my enemies; I take refuge in You.

PSALM 143:9, NASB

GOD IS A REFUGE from our enemies. Hannah proved this when a few years ago she was left widowed with four young children in an area of Pakistan that didn't have many Christians to begin with. From the start, it was hard to provide for her family, but then it got even harder. As her children became school aged, other children started picking on them because they were Christians. Hannah's son was often beaten up by other children. The parents of the other children encouraged the aggression, and they considered Hannah's children as outcasts in their society, polluting the purity of their Islamic culture.

Then the threats increased. The parents said they would kill Hannah and her son if they didn't move away. Hannah reported them to the police, but the police did nothing.

During that time of great fear, Hannah and her family found a verse of Scripture that became their refuge: "Be faithful unto death, and I will give you the crown of life" (Revelation 2:10, ESV). She and her children grew strong in their faith, knowing that if the worst were to happen, they would receive crowns in heaven. They understood the words of the apostle Paul that tell us not to set our eyes on what is seen, because it is temporary, but on what is unseen, because it's eternal (see 2 Corinthians 4:18).

The family was able to flee to a city with a stronger community of believers where things are easier, and—more important—where they no longer have to suffer alone and they can grow in their faith alongside others. They pray for those in their country who persecute Christians, for, as Paul says, "The god of this age has blinded the minds of unbelievers, so that they cannot see the light of the gospel that displays the glory of Christ" (2 Corinthians 4:4). They know our battle isn't against those who are spiritually blind. Our real battle is a spiritual battle that must be fought with prayer and God's Word, "for our struggle is not against flesh and blood, but against the rulers, against the authorities, against the powers of this dark world and against the spiritual forces of evil in the heavenly realms" (Ephesians 6:12).

Regardless of our circumstances, we always have a refuge in our Savior, who has already defeated our real enemy. God is our "ever-present help in trouble" (Psalm 46:1). The name of Jesus is a place of safety. "The name of the LORD is a fortified tower; the righteous run to it and are safe" (Proverbs 18:10). Even the Word of God is a refuge. "Every word of God is flawless; he is a shield to those who take refuge in him" (Proverbs 30:5). Let's make sure we don't spend too much time looking for solutions to our challenges in other places, and far too little time finding refuge in the truth of God's Word, in the power of prayer, and in the exercise of faith.

God, thank you for being a refuge for persecuted Christians around the world. Let your words, and your very name, be a source of strength to them today, whatever they may be facing. And Lord, please help me stay focused on who the real enemy is and to run to you, my place of refuge and safety, putting my whole trust in you, your Word, and your name. Thank you, Lord.

DAY 17

WALKING WORTHY

I, the prisoner of the Lord, implore you to walk in a manner worthy of the calling with which you have been called.

EPHESIANS 4:1, NASB

WANG MINGDAO is one of the most influential Christian leaders in Chinese history. In the early 1900s, he preached a pure gospel, not influenced by politics or theological trends, and built one of the largest churches in Beijing at the time—a congregation of 570 members.

After foreign missionaries were expelled, Wang stepped up to fill in the gap, and he began speaking and evangelizing throughout the nation. Wang was threatened so many times that he famously kept a coffin in his home, just in case. Yet, authorities continued to allow him to preach . . . for a time.

When Wang proclaimed, "We are ready to pay any price to preserve the Word of God," authorities took him at his word and arrested him. Under torture in prison, he broke down and signed a statement to join the "state church" that—at the time—denigrated Scripture.

Released from prison, but deeply grieved by his betrayal, Wang revoked his confession. His next arrest would be his last. Wang was incarcerated once again, enduring unending torture in prison for the next twenty-two years. In 1979, an eighty-year-old Wang emerged from prison, broken in body but stronger than ever in spirit, and he was overjoyed to discover that his own suffering had inspired countless thousands of Chinese pastors to fill in the gap he left while in prison, just as he had filled in the gap left by the expelled missionaries. The gospel was always on the move, never losing an inch.

Today we see persecution throughout the world much like what Wang endured, but we also continue to see the miraculous advance of the gospel. Many "Wangs" are emerging in their home countries as bold witnesses for Christ. Many "apostle Pauls" are preaching, being arrested and beaten, then preaching some more, only to be arrested again.

We are witnessing first-century Christianity in the twenty-first century, bringing a harvest of millions to Jesus. Persecuted or not, we also are to walk worthy of the calling given to us by Jesus Christ.

For Wang, "walking worthy" meant returning to the horrors of prison and decades of separation from his beloved family, his Bible, and his normal life. For most of us, following Jesus costs us so little, but one day it may cost us more. Let's practice obedience and walk worthy today.

Father, I am challenged by Pastor Wang's story. Please touch brave heroes like him around the world today, those who are suffering for the privilege of following the call of Christ. And please help me to do the same—not to settle for being a mediocre Christian but to walk in a manner that is worthy of the high calling of Christ. Thank you, Lord.

DAY 18

PRISON CHURCHES

I want you to know, brothers, that what has happened to me has really served to advance the gospel, so that it has become known throughout the whole imperial guard and to all the rest that my imprisonment is for Christ. And most of the brothers, having become confident in the Lord by my imprisonment, are much more bold to speak the word without fear.

PHILIPPIANS 1:12-14, ESV

ONE OF THE MOST POWERFUL experiences in my own life has been witnessing the miraculous stories in the New Testament actually happening in our world today. It seems there are more miracles among the persecuted than in any other group in our world, and those miracles appear in similar ways as they appeared in the early church.

In 1993, a house-church leader in China had a most unusual experience that brings to life the words of Paul to the Philippians: "What has happened to me has really served to advance the gospel" (Philippians 1:12, ESV).

Pastor Philip was arrested along with a group of believers in a government roundup. Because he was the leader, he was beaten almost to death with batons and cattle prods and kicked with steel-toed boots, which broke many of his bones. Guards then threw his unconscious body into a small cell that housed twenty-eight people. Because of Philip's injuries, even a hard-hearted criminal who had taken over the group of prisoners had mercy on him and placed Philip on the only bed in the cell.

In the middle of the night, the prisoners were shocked to see a light glowing around Philip. Even the guards saw it. All the prisoners stood back, terrified—that is, except Philip, who slept under a supernatural glow that lasted for several hours. The next morning, Philip awoke with his broken ribs and collarbone completely and miraculously healed.

One of the inmates asked, "Who are you?"

Philip smiled and said, "It doesn't matter who I am, but let me tell you about Jesus Christ."

Everyone in the cell then converted to Christianity.

It reminds me of the words of the psalmist: "You brought us into prison and laid burdens on our backs. You let people ride over our heads; we went through fire and water, but you brought us to a place of abundance" (Psalm 66:11-12).

What are you struggling with today? How can God use it to "advance the gospel" with those around you?

God, such beatings and persecution are hard to read about. Please be with those in the persecuted church today who are being arrested and treated so unjustly, and may you use their circumstances to advance your gospel. I also submit my life to you, and I trust that even in the most difficult moments, you will be present with me. May you do with me as you do with them, and let your light shine even when things are hard. Thank you, Lord.

DAY 19

PERSECUTION AND FULL CHRISTIANITY

When I am afraid, I will put my trust in you. I praise God for what he has promised. I trust in God, so why should I be afraid? What can mere mortals do to me?

PSALM 56:3-4, NLT

TURKEY IS A NATION rich in Christian history. The "Seven Churches of Asia" mentioned in Revelation are all located in modern Turkey: Ephesus, Smyrna, Pergamum, Thyatira, Sardis, Philadelphia, and Laodicea. But in 1453, Turkey came under the control of Islamic rule, and the predominantly Christian population dwindled.

One hundred years ago, 22 percent of Turkish citizens were Christians, but in 1922, persecution and genocide escalated. The Turkish army intentionally set the Great Fire of Smyrna. It was an attempt to drive out or kill Christians, including ethnic Greek and Armenian Christians. Historians estimate that one hundred thousand Christians were killed in the purge.

The Christian population never rebounded. Today, less than three-tenths of a percent of the population of Turkey follow Christ—fewer than two hundred thousand people nationwide—and the remaining Christians feel squeezed more and more every day. In 2017, for example, Turkey's president Recep Tayyip Erdogan confiscated thirty Christian properties in one weekend and authorized Islamic prayers to be held at the Hagia Sophia on the Muslim holy day of Eid. The Hagia Sophia not only is one of Christianity's most ancient and significant churches (and now a museum) but it was also once taken over and converted to a mosque. It seems Erdogan wants to do so again having already appointed a full-time Imam responsible for it.

Living under constant anxiety sounds dire, but for the two hundred thousand remaining Christians, it's the only world they know. These brave, isolated believers literally live out Psalm 9:13: "LORD, see how my enemies persecute me! Have mercy and lift me up from the gates of death." They live as King David wrote: "I trust in God, so why should I be afraid? What can mere mortals do to me?" (Psalm 56:11, NLT).

Learning to trust God is a hard lesson for any of us, but there must be special grace for isolated believers, like Turkish Christians, to trust the Lord and remain committed to him under such pressure. Coming from these circumstances, how shocking it must be for some Turkish Christians to see how many in the West profess Christ but take for granted our freedom and live with so little faith. We have so much and live with such doubt. They have so little and live with such faith.

The entire New Testament is filled with stories of Christian persecution; so much so that it seems nearly impossible to have the full Christian experience without proximity to the persecuted church. To experience the full Christian life when we are not being persecuted, we must keep close to the persecuted church. Getting close to the Turkish church is a way of doing that, but regardless, we must live with the persecuted church in mind—praying for them, supporting them, thinking of them.

Father, please protect the many persecuted believers who face constant threats. I pray with the psalmist that you would deliver them from their enemies and set them securely away from those who rise up against them. Deliver them from those who aim to do evil against them. And please help me to deepen my trust in you by being mindful of persecuted Christians.

DAY 20

EVEN THE CHILDREN

Faith is the substance of things hoped for,
the evidence of things not seen.

HEBREWS 11:1, NKJV

THE YOUNG IRAQI COUPLE loved Jesus, and they loved their church. In fact, they had helped to found St. George's Anglican Church in Baghdad, and they named their eldest son George, after the church. They then named their second son Andrew, after its pastor, Canon Andrew White.

It broke their hearts when they had to flee their home and the church that meant so much to them, but well-armed and well-funded ISIS fighters made it too dangerous for Christians to stay. The young parents took their small boys and joined tens of thousands of refugees to seek safety in another community. Yet as the evacuees arrived in the city, the forces protecting the city were overpowered by ISIS terrorists.

A bloodbath ensued, and the young parents tried to protect their children. But five-year-old Andrew drew the attention of a bloodthirsty and hate-filled jihadist who lifted his sword and literally cut the little boy in half. The stricken family had no time to grieve. They were forced to continue running with thousands of others, fleeing for their lives.

Little Andrew's death and the horror his agonized parents experienced made headlines, but their experience isn't an isolated one. Thousands of Iraqi Christians have endured similar terrible moments. Christians have been driven from their homes, losing all they owned and watching countless family members die. Money, homes, and possessions have been seized and have become the very funds used to arm and supply the jihadists who aimed to kill them.

When I recount these types of stories to American Christians, they often ask, perplexed, "How can these people still believe in God, having seen what they've seen and experienced what they've experienced?" Yet when I meet with Christians who've lost everything, they look at such questions with similar profundity, but their attitude is very different: "How can I not continue to believe in God? He's all I have, and he's always been with me."

I once spoke to an American who said to me, "So many of these Christians could just convert to Islam until the terrorists leave, and then they would live to preach another day!" Yet when you pose such an idea to Iraqi or Syrian Christians, they look at you totally perplexed and say, "How is it possible for me to convert?" They can't imagine such a thing. They are either Christians or they are not, and being a Christian costs something.

After the massacre, young Andrew's namesake, Canon Andrew White, requested prayer, and he specifically asked Christians to pray for "three Ps" for the persecuted church: protection, provision, and perseverance. It's a good thing for us to pray for the persecuted church every day.

Notice, though, he didn't ask for us to pray that they might have *faith*. In fact, they have all the faith in the world. Perhaps we ought to pray that *we* would have faith, for we already have all the protection and provision to help us persevere.

God, I believe Psalm 34:18, which says you are near to the broken-hearted and those crushed in spirit, so I pray for those who have had to flee from their homes and who have experienced unspeakable horror. I ask, along with this pastor, for you to give protection, provision, and perseverance to these Christian refugees. And please help me also to recognize how close you are, even in times of my greatest sorrow or discouragement.

DAY 21

THE WORLD WILL HATE US

Do not be surprised, brethren, if the world hates you.

1 JOHN 3:13, NASB

A YOUNG CHRISTIAN MAN outside of Lahore, Pakistan, just wanted to serve God. But when militants came to search his house, they started kicking his Bible around. He could endure the blows to his body, but he could not stand for them assaulting the Bible. He told his friends about the incident, and soon their entire Christian community banded together to protest that the police were insulting God's Word.

In response, the police incited the Muslim community to protest that the Christians were burning the Koran. (They weren't.) What started as simple protests quickly devolved into violence and then into an attempted massacre. Extremists burned churches and killed at least one pastor. Then they gathered together Christians from twenty-five villages, even from prison—two thousand in all. The extremists then looted and set fire to most of the Christians' houses. In all, 785 homes and 4 churches were burned to the ground. All of this because a few Christians raised their voices about their Bible being kicked around!

Before allowing the Christian families to return to their villages, the radicals stepped up the assault one more level and kidnapped their daughters and raped them repeatedly. Christians eventually rebuilt and settled into a very tense calm. The kidnapped girls eventually returned to their families, many of them after months of severe abuse.

The Christians have grown accustomed to being hated. They receive constant threats, both written and spoken, that they'll be burned again. Sometimes the threats are carried out.

Throughout extremist areas within the Islamic world, Christians who share God's Word, even just with each other, often are accused of blasphemy against Islam. They are arrested, and many serve severe prison sentences, even without any proof.

Yet as a result, Pakistani Christians say they are

increasing in their faith. They are in no way surprised by the hatred of their tormentors. They take literally the psalm, "Even though I walk through the valley of the shadow of death, I will fear no evil, for you are with me" (Psalm 23:4).

Our enemy hates Christians, hates Jesus, hates the Cross of Christ. Everyone who bears the name of Christ can *expect* to be hated. It's personal for the enemy. It reminds Satan that he has been defeated and will ultimately be held accountable for the evil he commits against God's children. Some Pakistani Christians are not surprised when they are hated. In fact, they are surprised when they go through a season of relative calm.

We can learn from their outlook. There's no reason to be surprised when we are misunderstood, taken to task, or hated for our Christian faith. On the contrary, we ought to expect no less, and when we are victims of it we ought to praise God that our faith was on display enough to merit the hatred.

God, I ask you to help the many displaced Christians whose houses and churches have been destroyed. Please give them the courage and the resources to rebuild, and show me how I can help them. Help me also to stop being surprised when people rebuke me or deliberately twist my words or attack my Christian witness. The enemy hates you and hates the Cross, so I hope my faith is strong enough that the enemy hates me as well. Help me to bear up under it and learn from the persecuted church to "fear no evil, for you are with me."

DAY 22

ATTACKED FOR NO REASON

Deliver me from my enemies, O my God; set me securely on high away from those who rise up against me. Deliver me from those who do iniquity and save me from men of bloodshed. For behold, they have set an ambush for my life; fierce men launch an attack against me, not for my transgression nor for my sin, O LORD.

PSALM 59:1-3, NASB

ONE DAY IN 2016, a seventy-four-year-old woman named Bridget bustled about selling plastic wares in an open-air market in Kano, Northern Nigeria, an area known for sectarian clashes and religious violence. Her husband, Mike, a pastor at a popular Pentecostal church, was with her. The two of them were ethnically Igbo people, who are almost all Christians and are easy to distinguish from other Nigerians.

For reasons unknown, five young Islamic extremists engaged Bridget in conversation. As they tried to convert her, she calmly let them know that she didn't agree with their views. The young men became agitated; then one punched her, and the others joined in the scuffle. Accusing her of insulting the prophet Muhammad, they increased their blows and brutally murdered Bridget in broad daylight. They reached for Mike, but the police arrived in time to save him from what was later described as "mob violence." The police no doubt feared the extremists too.

Muslims, Christians, and government officials alike condemned the attack, but in court the young men pleaded not guilty to murder and were acquitted and set free.

Many Muslims show respect for Christians, but persecution is spreading like a disease within the Islamic world. Most of the ancient Christian communities throughout the Middle East and North Africa are pacifist and do not believe in or practice violence. The people are law-abiding and peace-loving members of society who are not only good citizens but over-contributors to the economy. They have often been business owners, bankers, professors, doctors, lawyers, and accountants. The Christians in countries like Iraq and Syria made up the backbone of the economy.

They are used to being attacked for no reason except that their attackers have no room in their belief systems for anyone different from them.

The psalmist in our verse today describes being attacked

unjustly. Peter later echoes this, saying, “Dear friends, don’t be surprised at the fiery trials you are going through, as if something strange were happening to you” (1 Peter 4:12, NLT).

It shouldn’t surprise us when we are attacked without cause, when we are the subject of prejudice and discrimination, or when justice isn’t exercised on our behalf. Why would things be any different for us than they have been for many of our brothers and sisters over many centuries?

Christians have often called themselves sojourners and pilgrims and have referred to themselves as being “in the world but not of it” (see John 17:14-19) or “citizens of heaven” (see Philippians 3:20). These phrases are spread throughout the New Testament in various forms because the early Christians, almost all of whom faced discrimination and sometimes imprisonment and martyrdom, began to lower their expectations for their experience on earth. They couldn’t rely on the rule of law or on human rights. They had to recognize that they were just traveling through this earth on a mission from God, but their real home was in heaven.

In that sense, we have already been assured of absolute victory in the war we are fighting, because it is actually a spiritual war. Paul wrote, "The weapons we fight with are not the weapons of the world. On the contrary, they have divine power to demolish strongholds" (2 Corinthians 10:4).

The Holy Spirit's power within us is greater than dishonest judges or even the bloodlust of murderers. Unprovoked attacks may happen, but we are victors because we don't place our hope on what happens on this earth.

Dear God, please deliver people in the persecuted church who are innocent but are treated as guilty, and free them from the charges leveled against them. Lord, help me not to react to attacks against me personally, but help me to respond with Christian love and recognize that this is part of the cost of following you. Let me love those who are blinded to you. Help me to see opposition against me as an opportunity to be a witness of your grace to others.

DAY 23

MUSLIMS DREAM OF JESUS

I am the least of the apostles, unworthy to be called an apostle, because I persecuted the church of God. But by the grace of God I am what I am, and his grace toward me was not in vain. On the contrary, I worked harder than any of them, though it was not I, but the grace of God that is with me.

1 CORINTHIANS 15:9-10, ESV

TAHER BELIEVED he'd reached the pinnacle of his religious life on the day he completed his pilgrimage to Mecca and earned the right to wear the name "Hajji."

As a devout Muslim, he prayed regularly, observed fasts, memorized the Koran, and attended the *khutbah* every week before Friday prayers. Life seemed great . . . until his daughter converted to Christianity. Taher was outraged, then became murderous when his son, and even his wife, converted. He beat them and threatened to kill them. The family fled for their lives to another country.

Without his family, Taher thought he'd worship Allah in

peace. But peace didn't come. In his loneliness, he began to wonder about Christianity.

He had never heard from Allah, but his family had claimed to hear from God. That's when he made a decision to worship whichever god revealed himself. Soon after, he had a disturbing dream about a man on a donkey who said, "I will clean you from all your sins. Believe in me."

Later in the dream, someone said the man on the donkey was Jesus Christ, the one who "cleans your sins."

Taher awoke disturbed, but each time he fell back to sleep, the dream returned. The next day, he went to his family's church. There, believers took some time to determine that he wasn't a spy before they led him to Christ.

Today, Taher has rejoined his family and worships God together with them.

Taher's story sounds like a retelling of the story of Saul, who became the apostle Paul after he met Jesus in a blinding light on the road to Damascus. But Taher's testimony is not a one-off story. The Holy Spirit is moving among Muslims in powerful ways, producing a massive shift to Christianity in unprecedented ways. Almost every day there's another "Saul" transformed to "Paul" on the road to Damascus!

In the midst of the horrible persecution against Christians worldwide, our "secret weapons" of the gospel and the power of the Holy Spirit are at work. God is not finished with Muslims. He doesn't hate Muslims. God loves Muslims. As a result, Muslims are having dreams and visions in unprecedented numbers. One estimate is that 80 percent of Muslims who convert do so after having a dream in which God reveals himself.

Today will provide as great an opportunity as you'll ever have to pray for Muslim neighbors, coworkers, acquaintances, or those you simply see on the street. God is at work, creating an awakening that defies stereotypes of peoples or methods. We can join the movement to reach them by praying for God to continue these miraculous events.

The next time you walk past a Muslim neighbor, why don't you make it a point to immediately pray for them?

God, the story of Taher is so encouraging. Please continue to reveal yourself to Muslims through their dreams, their circumstances, their families, or any other creative ways. I pray that more and more Muslims will come to Christ. And Lord, help me remember to pray for the Islamic community. May the Muslim world know the joy of your salvation.

DAY 24

FEARLESS TO SHARE THE GOOD NEWS

The LORD is my light and my salvation—whom shall I fear? The LORD is the stronghold of my life—of whom shall I be afraid?

PSALM 27:1

THE MASSIVE SHRINE complex in Iran's holiest city, Mashhad, attracts twenty million Shiite pilgrims every year. Rami was born there to devout Muslim parents, but when he turned nine years old, his mother died, and he started wondering, *Where did Mama go when she died?*

At age fifteen, a friend shared the gospel with Rami. The friend gave him a New Testament, but still Rami did not convert. One day after reading the New Testament, Rami felt like taking a walk. He wandered aimlessly for more than five miles until he felt an urge to make a random stop at a house. To his surprise, his friend's pastor answered Rami's knock and said, "I've been waiting for you."

God had revealed to the pastor that Rami would come. That day, Rami had come, and he received Christ.

Persecution became an everyday occurrence for Rami, as it is for so many Iranian believers. When he was eighteen, the police began interrogating him. Then he was away in the military when his beloved pastor was executed. Three years later, he started preaching in his pastor's place. Repeatedly, the police interrogated him, and every time he felt a surge of God's power.

"Stop preaching to us!" the police demanded one time.

But he pressed his points with clear Scripture recall and said, "I'm just telling you about my own life."

In his late thirties, Rami felt led to leave his homeland. He has since planted Iranian churches in two countries, and he's always remembering the persecuted church. "Christians around the world need to be aware of those who are persecuted," he says.

Stop and think about this for a moment. Rami pastored a church for two decades in Iran's most holy Islamic city. We ask ourselves why our faith seems powerless and why we succumb so easily to fear. Maybe the religious freedom most of us enjoy keeps us from needing the power and fearlessness we have available to us in Jesus Christ.

That's only part of it, however, and it's the lesser part of it. For Rami, sharing Christ with others set the stage for God's power to show up. If we also shared the Good News of Jesus with others, then we might also know God's power for ourselves.

Dear Father, please give persecuted believers the courage and power they need to witness for you. Please give them wisdom to know when to stay or when to leave. Help me be inspired by them not to be shy in my own witness for Christ. Give me the courage and power I need as I open my mouth to share your love with others.

DAY 25

COMMUNISM'S SPIRITUAL BLINDNESS

In this you rejoice, though now for a little while, if necessary, you have been grieved by various trials, so that the tested genuineness of your faith—more precious than gold that perishes though it is tested by fire—may be found to result in praise and glory and honor at the revelation of Jesus Christ. Though you have not seen him, you love him. Though you do not now see him, you believe in him and rejoice with joy that is inexpressible and filled with glory, obtaining the outcome of your faith, the salvation of your souls.

1 PETER 1:6-9, ESV

COMMUNISM? STILL?

In the West, most people see the Communist threat as a mere whimper compared to terror groups like ISIS. But for millions of Christians, Communism is still very real. Its ideology remains the greatest perpetrator of Christian persecution the world has ever known.

Karl Marx, the father of Communism, is noted as saying that religion is the "opiate of the masses." Lenin added that "any religious idea, any idea of any God at all, any flirtation even with a God is the most inexpressible foulness." Joseph Stalin succeeded Lenin and took action on Marxist-Leninist philosophy by presiding over the deaths of fifteen million Russian Orthodox Christians, a half million other Orthodox Christian adherents, 1.2 million Roman Catholics, and a million Pentecostals and evangelicals.

How is it that such an insidious ideology could result in such atrocity? How could intelligent and educated people fall prey to it? How could such irrationality persist?

The apostle Paul answered the question when he wrote that "the message of the cross is foolishness to those who are perishing" (1 Corinthians 1:18). Brave Christians have always suffered at the hands of tormentors who could not comprehend their faith because they were spiritually blind.

Sometimes Christians think they can explain, argue, and debate their way into protection, religious freedom, or a better place in society. We sometimes think we can argue people into salvation.

The truth is that rationality is insufficient. Arguments have their limits. We must have the power of the Spirit on our side, for only that power can peel the scales off the eyes of those who do not believe.

We must pray and fast as much as we witness and preach. We need God's supernatural help to open blind eyes.

When one speaks about supernatural, Spirit-filled help, some might expect grand miracles. But in actuality this mysterious walk of faith that opens blind, Communist eyes looks more like a quiet, prayerful walk of faith than like Red Seas parting, visions in the middle of the night, and dead men being raised!

It is a walk of faith, not of sight, that faithfully trusts the Spirit's help to make the spiritually blind finally see.

Persecuted and misunderstood Christians maintain their faith not through one grand miracle after another. Rather, their steady, daily, persistent faith in the Jesus they know personally as Savior is stronger than the opposition from their persecutors, and it remains real even as it is ridiculed by society as fantasy.

The Bible says, "Though you have not seen [Jesus], you love him. Though you do not now see him, you believe in him and rejoice with joy that is inexpressible and filled with glory, obtaining the outcome of your faith, the salvation of your souls" (1 Peter 1:8-9, ESV).

We must pray in faith for God to open the blinded eyes of those who oppose our faith, especially within Communist regimes.

God, please help those persecuted Christians who are still suffering under Communist rule. Open the eyes of those who are blind, and help me to walk in faith myself. May I not try to argue or persuade people without praying and fasting for them first. May there be a day in our lifetime when the most anti-Christian, authoritarian nations on our planet are broken open with the light and love of Jesus.

DAY 26

JESUS FEELS WHAT WE FEEL

Since he himself has gone through suffering and testing,
he is able to help us when we are being tested.

HEBREWS 2:18, NLT

JESUS IS GOD *incarnate*. That word is used to describe how Jesus is both 100 percent God and 100 percent man. Here's why that's important.

As God, Jesus is all powerful. This means there's no challenge that you will ever face that is a challenge to him.

As man, Jesus feels as you do. This means that there's never a moment in life when you're praying to a God who doesn't understand what it feels like to be you.

The Bible also puts it this way: "This High Priest of ours understands our weaknesses, for he faced all of the same testings we do" (Hebrews 4:15, NLT). When Christians are ridiculed, shamed, or even physically abused, we pray to a God who knows the pain of those experiences.

Jesus was ridiculed even by his own family and friends, so he knows what it's like to be misunderstood (see Mark 6:4).

Jesus also knows what it's like to be persecuted. Religious persecution is what cost him his life. He was spit on, unjustly tried, whipped nearly to death, and then crucified because he was preaching a message the authorities didn't like. He was killed for his faith in God and his message of salvation because it was a threat to the ruling authorities.

Extremists to this day sometimes crucify Christians. They think crucifixion is the ultimate shame and act of persecution. Since Jesus knows what this pain is like, and since Jesus was a man and felt it himself, we often read of prayers by soon-to-be martyrs who say, "Jesus, you know what I'm feeling at this moment. Please be with me."

Toward the end of his life, the great martyr Dietrich Bonhoeffer, who died fighting Nazi repression, wrote, "Lord Jesus Christ, you were poor and in distress, a captive and forsaken as I am. You know all man's troubles; you abide with me when all men fail me; you remember and seek me; it is your will that I should know you and turn to you. Lord, I hear your call and follow; help me."

We can find some comfort from someone who has compassion for us, but how much more are we comforted by someone who has been where we've been and gone through what we've gone through. That person understands like no one else truly can.

When you lose a loved one or a job, when a crisis comes and everyone says they are praying for you, none of it means quite so much as hearing it from a person who has gone through the same thing too.

Jesus is a persecuted Savior. When you face what he has faced, he is with you in a special way. Every day your Savior is an empathetic King.

Dear God, thank you for being a suffering Savior. You know what it feels like to be those persecuted Christians who are in dire circumstances today. Thank you for the promise to be with them. Help and comfort them, I ask in Jesus' name. And thank you for feeling what I feel too. Whatever happens in my life today, I know you know what it feels like to be me.

DAY 27

GROWTH THROUGH MARTYRDOM

Do not be afraid of what you are about to suffer. I tell you, the devil will put some of you in prison to test you, and you will suffer persecution for ten days. Be faithful, even to the point of death, and I will give you the crown of life.

REVELATION 2:10

SOMALIA MIGHT be the most dangerous place in the world. Decades of conflict have gutted the country's infrastructure. Somalia's economy ranks dead last among all nations, and it isn't a matter of *if* you will experience a terrorist attack but *when.*

Billy was born into a religious family in Mogadishu. His father was a tribal and religious leader who had memorized the entire Koran. Out of curiosity, Billy started studying an English Bible alongside his Koran. After three years of study, he converted to Christianity. He learned a lot from Christian radio broadcasts from the Seychelles and

Kenya, and it was on the radio that he first heard the voice of another Somali who was a Christian.

Billy's family threatened him when he confessed his new faith. That was when he first began to understand the words of Paul in 2 Timothy 3:12: "Everyone who wants to live a godly life in Christ Jesus will be persecuted."

Six years after his conversion, Billy met his first Christian Somali. Together, as underground Christians, they gathered fourteen believers and started an underground church. A year later, Muslims discovered the growing Christian community and started persecution in earnest.

One of their church members, Liibaan, now a famed Somali martyr, was the first to be murdered. Then a doctor who attended the church was shot to death. An educator was kidnapped and executed. A Christian man and his Muslim wife were executed together in their bedroom. Another church member was taken off a bus and executed in broad daylight.

Twelve in all were murdered. None of the murderers were ever prosecuted.

Today, just two members have survived out of the original church of fourteen—Billy and one other. Billy escaped many attempts on his life before moving to another country.

From that base, he travels in and out of Somalia, planting and nurturing underground house churches. No longer are there only fourteen Christians in Mogadishu. The church is quietly growing, partly because of the testimony of those twelve who died for Christ.

Billy's prayer today is one we could all learn to emulate—to pray for the people who have hurt us. He prays, "May God grant that those murderers will come to see the light that Jesus Christ is Lord; may they ask Jesus Christ to forgive them of their sins."

Many of them will. Many of them have.

Father, I thank you for the lives of persecuted Christians who return to their home nations to lead their people to you. Please bless their efforts and reward them personally for their work. Please save the murderers who persecute Christians so that they, too, can one day know the joy of your salvation. May their testimonies bring many more to life and salvation than they have killed. Thank you for the impact a story like this has on me. Help me to pray for those who persecute me and to do all I can to lead others to you.

DAY 28

FORGIVENESS EVEN FOR GENOCIDE

When they hurled their insults at him, he did not retaliate; when he suffered, he made no threats. Instead, he entrusted himself to him who judges justly.

1 PETER 2:23

ARMENIANS ARE FOND of saying their nation was the first nation to declare itself Christian. Over centuries, through one invading force after another, Armenia's tenacious Christian culture held fast, but Armenians eventually became a Christian minority living under the Muslim rule of Ottoman Turkey.

The Ottoman Turkish rulers were ruthless. President John Quincy Adams wrote of them, "Treachery and violence are taught as principles of religion." A century later, President Grover Cleveland wrote, "We have been afflicted by continued and not infrequent reports of the wanton destruction of homes and the bloody butchery of men, women and children, made martyrs to their profession of Christian faith."

In the late 1800s, Turkey conducted anti-Christian pogroms, slaughtering as many as three hundred thousand Armenian Christians. Two decades later, the government secretly completed the job while the world was focused on World War I. They tricked Armenians into giving up their arms, then encouraged the men to leave their homes and enlist in the military, only to slaughter them when they reported for duty. They promised to relocate the women and children "for protection" but sent them on a forced march through the desert to Syria. Most did not survive. Decaying corpses covered the roads. Concentration camps sprang up along the route, in which most inhabitants died. In all, 1.5 million Christians were killed.

It was genocide.

In fact, Adolf Hitler used the Armenian genocide as his example for eradicating Jews. He famously said, "Who, after all, speaks today of the annihilation of the Armenians?"

Beatrice is one Armenian girl who survived, but she still remembers the terrible thirst, the dying bodies, the rapes, and the cruelty. Nevertheless, she follows the biblical injunction, "Beloved, never avenge yourselves, but leave it to the wrath of God, for it is written, 'Vengeance is mine, I will repay, says the Lord'" (Romans 12:19, ESV). Beatrice in her old age says she has "no hard feelings." About her captors, she is quoted as saying, "They are human beings too."

We normally have a hard time forgiving someone who slights or disrespects us. But God calls us to a higher standard—to trust his justice.

World-famous Armenians today include Cher, William Saroyan, Andre Agassi, and the Kardashians. But the most famous Armenians in heaven are written in God's Book of Life, the millions who received crowns after being martyred for their faith.

God, it is difficult for me when people insult or hurt me, yet I can't imagine how difficult it is for persecuted Christians to forgive others when they watch people killing their loved ones and even trying to wipe out their people. Please help those who are persecuted to entrust themselves to you to bring justice. Help persecuted Christians today find a place of forgiveness and peace. And, Lord, I also forgive everyone who has hurt me, stolen from me, or tried to destroy me. I entrust myself to you, I entrust justice to you, and I even entrust them to you. God, please help them, and help me. Thank you for being just.

DAY 29

IMPRISONED MORE THAN FREE

Suffer hardship with me, as a good soldier of Christ Jesus.

2 TIMOTHY 2:3, NASB

"HARDSHIP" is a relative term. For a billionaire, financial hardship could mean you're down to your last million dollars. To the homeless, hardship could mean your bicycle was stolen. For a Chinese evangelist named Liu, hardship meant separation from loved ones, imprisonment, and torture.

The first time Liu was arrested for "disturbing social order," it was because she and some ministry partners were traveling from village to village teaching about Christ. "The police . . . asked a lot of information about my pastor and my friends," she said. "They ask me [to] give up Jesus Christ. [I said], 'I don't want to do that.' So, they beat me and they used the electric bar, an electric baton, that can shock your body and burn your skin.

"They put it to my head, my body, everywhere. And then they put it into my hands. It is painful. I was screaming. Then they put the baton in my mouth, so my whole mouth is so hurt, and I couldn't drink, couldn't eat and couldn't talk. They still asked information. And then, they give me shock chains on my ankles.

"No bathroom, no drink, no break. My whole faith was worn so very badly. I believe in Jesus, but my physical body feels so painful. When I fall down on the floor, then they yank me up and spin me around, hold my hair and lift me up from the ground. . . . They use their feet to smash my hands. . . . [But] I think about Jesus dying for me, and I [can] die for Him."

Liu was finally released, but five years later she was arrested again and sentenced to three more years in a labor camp. She was released, and five years later arrested again, this time for committing a "crime against the state." She won an appeal, but local police kidnapped her and put her back in a women's labor camp. But Liu was clear about her purpose. "My purpose is to share Gospel with people, even in prison," Liu said.

She lived what the apostle Paul wrote: "At the same time, pray also for us, that God may open to us a door for the word, to declare the mystery of Christ, on account of which I am in prison" (Colossians 4:3, ESV).

What does being a "good soldier" look like for us in the West? Almost certainly more than our present experience.

Father, please help these heroic Christians who are facing so much more than a momentary discomfort or an inconvenience. Help them to endure the hardships they face. Bless them. And help me to soldier on for you. Show me what you want me to do today, and help me to do it even if it is uncomfortable, even if it seems like a hardship.

DAY 30

TWO ROWS BY THE SEA

Love your enemies, do good to those who hate you.

LUKE 6:27

WHO CAN FORGET the 2015 scene of twenty-one Coptic Christian men lined up on a beach in Libya, their heads hanging, as masked ISIS swordsmen prepared to murder them by decapitation? Millions around the world shuddered at the sight. But Christians in Egypt didn't waste a minute. They sprang into action.

Following the injunction to "do good to those who hate you," they didn't take to the streets in protest or plot revenge. Instead, their inspired idea was to act quickly and write, design, and print a gospel tract called "Two Rows by the Sea."

On the cover, a picture of the row of Christians dressed in orange is flanked by the row of murderers dressed in black. Scriptures about blessing amid suffering are listed inside, with an Arabic poem that reads:

Who fears the other?
The row in orange, watching paradise open?
Or the row in black, with minds evil and broken?

The outrageous murders backfired, causing most Egyptians to become more softhearted toward Christians. As if to heighten that sentiment, the Egyptian Christians then did the unthinkable—they drew attention to themselves, not as helpless victims but by publicly forgiving the killers.

Within a week, the Bible Society of Egypt had distributed 1.65 million copies of the "Two Rows by the Sea" tract. It became their most successful campaign and showed how open Egypt had become to Christian materials.

A large church on one of Cairo's busiest streets went even further. They hung a banner with the Egyptian flag, and over it the words "We learn from what the Messiah has said: Love your enemies, do good to those who hate you."

It is next to impossible to imagine ourselves in the situation the families of those murdered men faced. Loss, grief, economic hardship, and fear followed the murders. Yet, in the midst of it all, God's peace and joy guided them as they forgave their enemies. One of the widows famously said, "Please don't worry about us. Jesus will take care of us."

In death, those twenty-one men helped propel an entire nation toward the gospel of Jesus Christ.

Lord, let those twenty-one deaths turn into millions of decisions for you, I pray. Help me be more quick to think of how to love an enemy than how to seek revenge. And please work in the hearts of every non-Christian who looks with awe at the love of Jesus through the lives of those who follow him. Draw them to you.

DAY 31

PRAY, THEN PRAY SOME MORE

Among God's churches we boast about your perseverance and faith in all the persecutions and trials you are enduring.

2 THESSALONIANS 1:4

SEVENTY-YEAR-OLD Hae-Woo has been a Christian now for fifteen years. She was led to Christ by her husband, who was eventually murdered in a hard-labor camp he was sent to because of his faith.

"Seeing my husband keep his faith even under such pain and suffering . . . was the key reason that I decided to become a Christian," she says. But she adds, "Living life as a Christian in North Korea was a living hell."

Worldwide, North Korea often ranks first in Christian persecution. North Korean propaganda is absolute. No other media is allowed into the country. Children are taught from an early age to fear Christian missionaries because they infect children with germs through needles.

Nevertheless, missiologists estimate the underground church in North Korea has as many as four hundred thousand Christian members. Another seventy thousand Christians are believed to be in labor camps. Others have been executed, because the punishment for evangelizing is death. If someone is caught with a Bible or in worship, the punishment extends to the entire family.

"I knew that becoming a Christian was extremely dangerous," Hae-Woo says. "It could take away not only my life, but my entire family's lives."

Twice Hae-Woo escaped the country, only to be sent back and arrested. In prison, she was once tortured for four days and thought she was going to die. She endured it only because she "thought about the suffering that Jesus had to go through on the cross."

She knew she had to sacrifice herself in prison for the sake of others, so she shared her meager food and her faith with inmates. Five people came to Christ under her ministry.

Today, Hae-Woo lives in another country. North Korea is known to extend its reach outside its borders in order to silence detractors, but Hae-Woo risks talking about North Korea to encourage others to pray. She lives out the words "among God's churches we boast about your perseverance and faith in all the persecutions and trials you are enduring."

Hae-Woo says today, "I want people to pray for my people in North Korea . . . and how I was blessed in the darkest moment in my life."

Some Christians have visited North Korea on tourist visas to pray from within the country for God to save its people. Yet, it's embarrassing how few prayers the global church offers for North Korea. With so many people suffering and the gospel under such oppression, we ought not let a single day go by when tens of millions of Christians aren't praying for North Korea. Instead, when we speak of the country, we speak of it only in political or militaristic terms. We talk about its volatility and its pursuit of nuclear weapons. We fear its erratic leader.

Yet, I've sometimes wondered if we would have so many problems with North Korea and other countries that persecute Christians if the church was more interested in praying than in discussing and fearing the geopolitical realities in our world.

Maybe North Korea's real problem is that the church in the free world offers the church in the suffering world too little support.

God, thank you for helping us who are outside North Korea to understand a little better what it's like inside that country. Please sustain the brave North Korean Christians, help them to multiply, and allow non-Christians to be drawn to them so they can also experience your salvation. Help us also to pray through the daily headlines and recognize our sacred responsibility to be lights in this very dark world.

DAY 32

READY WHEN THE DOOR OPENS

Blessed is the man who remains steadfast under trial, for when he has stood the test he will receive the crown of life, which God has promised to those who love him.

JAMES 1:12, ESV

US OFFICIALS ESTIMATE the population of North Korea to be roughly twenty-four million people. Missiologists believe that before the Korean War, 13 percent of the population was Christian; but today, at most, 2 percent are Christian. Kim Eun Jin is one. The thirty-one-year-old was born in Pyongyang, North Korea, into a rarity—a Christian family.

As a child in school, Kim was taught the official "truth" that there is no God and that people should worship the country's leaders. But growing up, she also heard that her hometown was once known as the "Jerusalem of the East" because of its great base of Christianity. On Saturday nights, her family continued the legacy. They gathered in the back of their tiny apartment and whispered their worship and Bible studies. "We often covered our heads to muffle the noise," she says.

Kim's grandmother had converted before World War II and had kept a Chinese Bible. It was their most prized possession. Kim's mother translated it by hand into Korean.

Those precious pages held the family together. Kim's father always reminded the family that they would pay a price one day for their Christianity. He often said, "Even if I face death I will follow Jesus." Each morning, he would hug Kim and remind her to be careful that day.

Every day, again and again, he gave her that hug and that warning.

Eventually, Kim's father was discovered. The police arrested him and an uncle on a day when Kim was at school. She never saw her father again, and she is now certain he is dead.

Kim, her mother, grandmother, and siblings all eventually escaped North Korea. Today, she is married and has a child and is frequently invited to speak to groups about human-rights abuses in North Korea.

"I grew up in a land where they said there was no God,"

she said in a recent interview. “But my father told me otherwise. He loved Christ and for that he died.” Her dream is to return to Pyongyang to share the love of Christ. “We are getting ready for that day when the doors open,” she says.

Kim had to endure a terrible trial, including the arrest and presumed death of her godly father. Far from waiting around for the day when she will receive her crown in heaven, she is actively going about the Lord’s work. She especially is not letting go of the belief that she will one day see her homeland of North Korea turn toward Christ.

Many Koreans feel the same. They are praying and preparing for that day, and they believe wholeheartedly that it will come. I’m wondering if we have such faith. May we have faith that one day all the closed doors and persecuted places will spring forth with the beautiful gospel of Jesus Christ.

May we pray and work till that day comes.

God, thank you for safely bringing Kim out of North Korea so the rest of the world will know how to pray. I join my voice with hers today and ask you, Lord, to bring about a change in North Korea. Cause the Christians to multiply so their numbers cannot be ignored. Give the persecuted church great boldness, and please shield them from their government, so they can share the love of Christ with others. And please help me to be just as steadfast myself, praying for my unsaved friends and loved ones and trusting you with my own life. May there be a day when the worship of your name sounds in the streets across that closed-off place.

DAY 33

ALWAYS READY FOR MARTYRDOM

God has not given us a spirit of fear, but of power and of love and of a sound mind.

2 TIMOTHY 1:7, NKJV

THE RUTHLESS UGANDAN dictator Idi Amin once famously ordered soldiers to machine-gun down whole herds of elephants. He wasn't any less ruthless toward Uganda's Christians.

The sadistic military general seized control of the country in 1971 and promised reform. The first "reform" was to wipe out perceived enemies. Illiterate and uneducated, Amin would issue orders verbally to illiterate soldiers who tried to memorize what he said, under fear of reprisals if they didn't carry out the dictator's decrees. His perceived enemies kept increasing in number. Asians were expelled for "sabotaging" the economy. Then twenty-seven Christian denominations were banned because he claimed they posed a threat to his authority.

During this time, Ben Oluka became the senior assistant secretary in the Department of Religious Affairs for Amin. His job was to ensure that Amin's church ban was carried out. Tens of thousands of Christians fled the country to an uncertain and an often unwelcome future in neighboring countries. Eighty percent of Ugandans were Christians at the time, meaning millions more were trapped at home. The church immediately went underground.

Among the underground churches formed was one pastored by none other than Ben Oluka.

Ben worked as a double agent, aiding Christians as he could and jamming the government's efforts to wipe out churches, all while appearing to do his job. It was scary business. Amin killed on a whim. Nightly, armed guards prowled through neighborhoods, kidnapping people at random and taking them to a killing field where the guards tortured, shot, or burned them alive.

Ben says, "I was personally ready for martyrdom."

Ugandan Christians refused to give in to a spirit of fear. They bound together to pray for an end to the bloodshed. The Christians who were expelled worked hard to evangelize in the countries where they went. Although jobless and near starvation themselves, many found a way to send support to their loved ones trapped at home.

Grabbing hold of the spirit "of power and of love and of a sound mind," the determined Christians outlasted Amin, who was overthrown after eight bloody years and fled to Libya, then died in Saudi Arabia.

Amin's cruel dictatorship will long be remembered, but the faithful Christians of Uganda will be remembered eternally, as they endured severe persecution and saw the Lord restore their nation. When I last went to Uganda, I saw a church that was thriving. It was beautiful and alive, and it was on the move. Amin inadvertently motivated an entire generation of Ugandan Christians who were, as I wrote about in *The Martyr's Oath*, willing to die for a Jesus most Christians in other parts of the world were barely willing to live for. Now they are leading a church in revival.

As in many African countries, Christians are still persecuted on occasion in Uganda, but the Christian story in the country has drastically changed. The church in Uganda is no longer a bleeding church but a building church. It's no longer a battered church but a blessed church. The people are finding in Jesus faith and hope that heals and saves.

As Romans 16:20 says, “The God of peace will soon crush Satan under your feet.” God and his people will have the last say and the ultimate victory.

God, please help those in the persecuted church worldwide to stand strong as these Ugandans did. Please give them courage and strength today. And let this story penetrate my heart and motivate me to stand strong against what I face, not giving in to fear but holding on to power, love, and a sound mind. May the story of Uganda's revival play itself out again and again in isolated, persecuted places the world over. Thank you, Jesus.

DAY 34

"BELIEVERS OF THIS CALIBER"

He rescued me from my powerful enemy, from my foes, who were too strong for me. They confronted me in the day of my disaster, but the LORD *was my support. He brought me out into a spacious place; he rescued me because he delighted in me.*

PSALM 18:17-19

IN THE NEARLY two hundred years since missionary David Livingstone witnessed his one convert in Africa, African Christians have repeatedly proven the strength of their faith. Ugandan Christians in particular have weathered more than a few disasters, and their faith has shone through it all. Journalist Dan Wooding reported just such an incident that occurred in 1978, during the reign of the bloody dictator Idi Amin.

Wooding spoke with Christians from a church in the city of Makerere who related how "wild-eyed soldiers" stormed the church and began firing bullets. The assistant pastor in the pulpit, Jotham Mutebi, dropped to his knees, and six hundred members followed, kneeling between the pews and raising their voices in prayer. A member of the church orchestra, Joseph Nyakairu, grabbed his trumpet and began to play. The church was filled with the noise of bullets, prayers, and trumpet blasts.

The soldiers, fearing the Christians were about to counterattack, ran away.

After the soldiers left, four hundred of the Christians also left while another two hundred stayed in the church and continued worshiping. But soon, the soldiers returned and arrested the two hundred worshipers, who were taken to jail to await execution orders expected to be issued by General Mustafa Adrisi, second in command to Idi Amin.

While the believers were praying, the general was involved in a terrible car crash that left him unable to sign the orders.

Many of the two hundred were eventually tortured, but because the execution orders never came, all were finally released. Wooding said, "I've never met believers of this caliber. . . . They certainly have much to teach us about faith and courage."

In today's Christian culture, we can be distracted from

having the perseverance, not to mention the fortitude, of the Ugandan Christians' faith in the face of the soldiers' threats to their lives. Demands of our fast-paced lifestyles and the temptation to pursue what the world claims is valuable can tempt us to quit too easily, love too little, and think too small. Most of us don't prioritize fighting for the salvation of others and don't often willingly sacrifice great things.

There aren't a lot of us these days who would give up our Western comforts and conveniences and persevere in the face of certain defeat. Many of us can't fathom remaining in a culture that is so dangerous to our faith. The Ugandan Christians echo a lesson from a pastor in the Islamic nation of Tunisia. He pointed to an olive grove and said, "It takes a generation or two for olive trees to bear fruit. You plant an olive grove for your children or your grandchildren's benefit. That's also how the gospel works its way into hard places. I'm investing my entire life for a revival I will probably never see, but I know it'll come."

That mind-set obviously took root in the lives of Christians in Uganda.

Father, help those living for you in the most difficult places in the world, and thank you for those who've gone before us doing the same. Please help me follow their example, regardless of whether we see the fruits of our efforts this side of heaven. And free me of living for the here and now. Help me to have the faith to persevere for the benefit of future generations. May I work for you harder than I work for myself. May I love others as I want to be loved and as you've loved me. May I have the conviction to live like the gospel is the most important thing in the world. And may I pour myself into it even if I never see the fruit of my work.

DAY 35

RIGHTEOUS PEOPLE STILL ACT

Greater love has no one than this, that someone lay down his life for his friends.

JOHN 15:13, ESV

GERMAN NAZIS under Adolf Hitler murdered six million Jews. Historians estimate that at least another five million more non-Jews were killed as well, including many Christian pastors who resisted the rise of the Nazis or who attempted to save the Jews being marched off to gas chambers.

Three thousand Catholic priests from Poland alone were killed during the war years from 1939 to 1945. One of them was Poland's Maximilian Kolbe, a priest whom the Roman Catholic Church declared to be a saint in 1982.

Father Kolbe was born in 1894 to Polish and German

parents. He went into the ministry in his twenties and founded monasteries in Poland, Japan, and India. During the German invasion, he hid Jews and thousands of refugees in his monastery. He also operated newspapers and radio broadcasts. His message was clear: "The real conflict is the inner conflict. Beyond armies of occupation and the hecatombs of extermination camps, there are two irreconcilable enemies in the depth of every soul: good and evil, sin and love."

In 1941, soldiers shut down Father Kolbe's operation and sent him to Auschwitz. When three prisoners vanished from the camp, guards selected ten prisoners to starve to death as a reprisal. One of the men chosen cried out for mercy since he had a family, so Father Kolbe offered to take his place.

As the ten men died, Father Kolbe led them in prayers and songs that sometimes became so loud that the prisoners didn't even notice the guards coming through. One by one, the men perished, but Father Kolbe remained alive, steadfast. After two frustrating weeks with their inmate who wouldn't die, the guards finally killed Father Kolbe by lethal injection.

Father Kolbe didn't have to become involved in rescuing

Jews, but he chose to because it was the right thing to do. It was the *righteous* thing to do.

Sometimes as Christians we suffer because we speak up for righteousness and act upon righteousness when the rest of the world is either complicit or indifferent. In the end, we may suffer the same fate as those we aim to save because we must put ourselves in harm's way to save them. Christians rush in when the world rushes out.

Jesus himself said to us, "Your care for others is the measure of your greatness" (Luke 9:48, TLB). Father Kolbe was a hero, but his heroic actions would have been within the power of us all. They are even within our power today. We can choose to do what's right when others turn away or turn against the truth.

Greatness starts by living as Christ taught: caring for others, and especially for those others hate.

Father, thank you for the love of Jesus as he laid down his life for mine. Please be with those in the persecuted church today who are laying down their lives for others. Give them strength and grace, and let their lives be a living witness of your love. Lord, I'd like to think that I would do the same in their position, but I need help in showing your love to others. Help me to always stand up for righteousness, and show me ways I can rush in when the world runs away.

DAY 36

THE TOUGHER THEY ARE, THE STRONGER WE BECOME

Jesus said, "Father, forgive them, for they do not know what they are doing."

LUKE 23:34

FOR SEVENTY YEARS in the atheistic Soviet Union, Christians were executed or imprisoned. Many were placed in a labor camp system called the "Gulag," famously chronicled by the dissident writer, Aleksandr Solzhenitsyn.

In the 1980s, at the end of unrelenting Soviet persecution, the general assumption was that Christianity had retreated, exactly as the government intended.

However, historians have since noted that Christianity actually *grew*.

A similar thing happened earlier in Russia's history. The official 1910 census showed fewer than two million Russians involved in "religious organizations," but a secret 1923 census counted more than three million. The difference is likely much greater than reported, because in 1910 Christianity wasn't yet outlawed, but by the 1923 census, people were risking their lives to confess religious involvement. So millions more could simply have been afraid to admit to their faith in the 1923 census.

Today, Russian Christians are still a small percentage of the population, but their numbers are rapidly growing and now make up at least 20 percent of the population.

What has caused this kind of growth?

A Russian linguist once noted the lasting impact of once-imprisoned Christians among other inmates: "Many prisoners observed that their Christian comrades had strength in their faith and [they] yearned to share in that hope and comfort [themselves]." In fact, Christians were so revered by the hardened criminals they were imprisoned with that in many instances the prison guards asked the Christians to help care for and educate the criminals.

In the Soviet Gulag system, survivors were generally those who felt they were "shar[ing] Christ's sufferings" (1 Peter 4:13, ESV), and they survived at a higher rate. By surviving, they extended their witness to prisoners and guards who would come and go.

Solzhenitsyn describes the Christians' self-confidence as "a steadfastness unheard of in the twentieth century." He says Christians "knew very well *for what* they were serving time, and they were unwavering in their convictions! They were the only ones, perhaps, to whom the camp philosophy did not stick."

Another author records the story of Father Tavrion Batozsky, who spent three decades in Soviet prisons and camps. He once said of that season in his life, "If you only knew how grateful I am [to] God for my wonderful life!"

When asked about his sunny attitude after being imprisoned unjustly and tortured, Father Roman Braga of Romania summarized what many Christian prisoners have said in different ways: "God bless [the torturers], if there are still alive some of them. I forgave them at that time. . . . Jesus on the Cross forgave them. . . . They don't know what they do. . . . We forgive them because we want them to come to God and become people."

Solzhenitsyn also recounts the story of an elderly woman who was interrogated repeatedly in the hope she would reveal the identity of a particular priest in the prison.

She finally blurted to the guards, "There is nothing you can do with me even if you cut me into pieces. After all, you are afraid of your bosses, and you are afraid of each other, and you are even afraid of killing me. . . . But I am not afraid of anything. I would be glad to be judged by God right this minute."

Every time the Soviets dialed up the intensity, they only strengthened the resolve of those they aimed to silence, like stone hardened under years of pressure. So Christianity survived the Soviet Union and now thrives in Russia itself and in countless other countries that were once held under its authoritarian control.

In the words of a Protestant Reformer, "The Bible is an anvil which has worn out many a hammer."

God, please help the Christians who are in prison today for their faith. Sustain them, strengthen them, and make them a light to others. Help them to be a witness to other inmates and to their prison guards. May their testimonies spark a revival even among those who aim to destroy them, and may I have the same resolve with my own faith. May every ounce of pressure only strengthen my faith. Thank you, Lord.

DAY 37

HE ALWAYS HEARS AND ACTS

The LORD hears the needy and does not despise his own people who are prisoners.

PSALM 69:33, ESV

IN NIGERIA TODAY, Boko Haram militants travel from village to village specifically looking to kill and kidnap Christians and destroy churches. The Boko Haram leaders of Northern Nigeria are clear—they intend to wipe Christians off the face of the planet.

For years, Boko Haram has outpaced ISIS in both brutality and body count. Because of that, Northern Nigeria is the front line in the battle between Christianity and extreme Islam in Africa. The way the world turns a blind eye to Boko Haram's barbaric escapades is an international embarrassment, but for some families, it's a personal disaster.

A pregnant mother of six, whom we'll call Violet, lived in a village that was sacked by Boko Haram. Her husband was taken prisoner. Violet led her children into the mountains and found safety at first in a cave. She baked edible grasses to keep the children's hunger at bay. Finally, she set out again, praying she could get to the border. For two harrowing days, she walked her family to a UN refugee camp in Cameroon.

After two months, Violet decided to go back to Nigeria to have her baby, hoping her husband might still turn up. She led her children through the mountains for days, until their feet were bruised and swollen, and she feared they would all die. The little family came to what looked like a safe camp, but Violet realized she and her children were the only Christians, so she led them away. Going from camp to camp, Violet finally found a primitive Christian camp with church leaders who embraced her family. There she gave birth to her baby. Compounding the joy of new birth, word finally reached her that her husband was alive.

When Violet's husband rejoined his family, he recounted how he'd been beaten and witnessed terrible murders. Nigerian soldiers threatened Boko Haram at one point, giving him and other Christians the opportunity to make their escape. They barely stayed ahead of the terrorists. He saw many tortured people, burned churches, and destroyed houses. Some who fled with him were killed, and others died of exhaustion. For six months, he hid in the hills before he found the camp in Cameroon, only to learn Violet and the children had gone back to Nigeria.

He rejoined his wife and children just after the birth of his seventh child.

This family has faced the reality of a physical enemy that is out to destroy Christians. In their distress, they were sheltered by our merciful God, who hears our cries and does not forsake us. Each day, we all face the enemy of our souls, who wants to steal, kill, and destroy us (see John 10:10). Our first line of defense is what Violet found as her last hope—*prayer.*

It was a miracle the family found one another again. It was God's grace at work in the midst of terror, murder, and pain. Rwanda's most famous Christian leader, Bishop John Rucyahana, posed an answer to the question "Where was God when a million Rwandans were killed in the genocide?" He wrote, "I'll tell you where God was. He was alongside the victims lying on the cold stone floor. . . . He was comforting a dying child. He was crying at the altar. But He was also saving lives. Many were saved by miracles. God does not flee when evil takes over a nation. He speaks to those who are still listening, He eases the pain of the suffering, and He saves those who can be saved. Man has free will, and God will not override it. . . . Even then, God does not abandon them."

God uses every prayer, even those we offer across the world, on behalf of his people facing terrible situations. Let us not neglect praying for our brothers and sisters in harm's way.

Lord God, please help the persecuted Christians who are being hunted and tormented by extremists today. Keep them safe. Cause their enemies to overlook them, to be blind to them. Help whole families to go unnoticed and be able to escape. And please help me to be more diligent in my prayer life, to fight the spiritual fight against the enemy and intercede for those who are needy and in prison. Thank you, Lord.

DAY 38

LONELY BUT NEVER ALONE

Because he holds fast to me in love, I will deliver him;
I will protect him, because he knows my name.

PSALM 91:14, ESV

FOR MANY IN AFGHANISTAN, to be an Afghan is to be a Muslim. There is no distinction.

The Afghan national identity *is* their religion. If you are no longer a Muslim, you can no longer be an Afghan. This paradox led a *New York Times* reporter to chronicle the fate of a Christian convert named "Josef," who is in hiding from both a government that would at worst execute him and at best deport him, and his family—uncles and in-laws—who are out to kill him for the sake of Islam.

Josef has a medical degree, but as a young husband and father, he drove a taxi to make ends meet. One day, Josef witnessed the shooting of an innocent child, an event that caused him to question his religion. Eventually, he forsook Islam, and he knew he had to leave the country because of it. His wife returned to her family in Pakistan while Josef worked extra hours and borrowed money to get to Europe.

Josef ended up wandering from country to country to gain asylum, without success. During a stopover in Hanover, Germany, he attended a church. "When I threw away my Islamic beliefs, I was living in a space of spiritual emptiness," he said. "I think I was impressed by the personality of Jesus himself. The fact that he came here to take all of our sins, that moved me. I admired his character and personality long before I was baptized."

Josef converted to Christianity during his short stay in Hanover. Eventually, German authorities arrested and deported Josef. Without proper paperwork, money, or a place to go, Josef went to Pakistan to reunite with his wife and son, but now he was a man with a deep secret. He carried a flash drive with digital copies of his asylum paperwork and the record of his baptism. His in-laws discovered the flash drive and beat him. They threatened to kill him. Josef narrowly escaped and made his way back home to Afghanistan.

Josef's brother-in-law followed him, determined to kill Josef and his three-year-old son to save the family's honor. The reporter quoted the brother-in-law saying, "If I find [Josef], once we are done with him, I will kill his son as well, because his son is a bastard. He is not from a Muslim father."

When he was interviewed, Josef was living in hiding in a crumbling basement outside of Kabul. He had a blue Bible he would read for comfort and was resolute in his decision to follow Christ. Perhaps he had read Psalm 91:14 (ESV): "Because he holds fast to me in love, I will deliver him; I will protect him, because he knows my name."

Josef told the reporter, "I inherited my faith, but I saw so many things that made me discard my religious beliefs. . . . When I threw away my convictions, it was hard to speak with people about it. It was like an imaginary prison. Now it is the other way around. My body is in prison, but my soul is free. . . . Even if I get killed, I won't convert back."

The apostle Paul writes, "He delivered us from such a deadly peril, and he will deliver us. On him we have set our hope that he will deliver us again" (2 Corinthians 1:10, ESV).

Josef's life makes this passage come to life for us. Afghans live with the knowledge that Christian converts are beaten and even sexually abused when arrested, then executed. Theirs is a nation of poverty and hardship that no number of military or political solutions have been able to save. It is up to us as Christians to pray for God's solution for people like Josef, who willingly suffer for Jesus every day, often without the support of friends or family.

If you ever feel alone, remember Josef and pray for Afghans who so desperately need the love of our Savior.

God, please deliver the people of Afghanistan who are held in such bondage. Make a way for Afghan converts, that they may be delivered and become witnesses to their people. Please be with them in lonely times, and help them to hold fast to you in love. Protect them and deliver them. And during times when I feel alone, help me know you are with me, and remind me to pray for others.

DAY 39

BLESSINGS THROUGH IMPRISONMENT

He delivered us from such a deadly peril, and he will deliver us. On him we have set our hope that he will deliver us again.

2 CORINTHIANS 1:10, ESV

MANY WORDS SPRING to mind when we hear the word *Sudan*. Civil war . . . refugees . . . terrorists . . . famine . . . slavery.

The Islamic nation boasts one of the longest recorded civil wars in history, a devastated infrastructure, and millions of hopeless citizens. Once the largest country in Africa, Sudan separated from South Sudan in 2011 and adopted Sharia law. By this time, more than two million people had been killed or enslaved in the decades of violent conflict.

Yet, in the midst of the darkness, a light shined.

Peter was from South Sudan and converted to Christianity as a child, growing up to become a pastor in the Presbyterian Evangelical Church. He went to Khartoum during the civil war. Another Christian, Michael, was a pastor's son who fled to Uganda when the war broke out. He later returned to Khartoum with his wife and children.

In Khartoum, a sermon Michael preached at the Bahari Evangelical Church was recorded and turned over to officials, who arrested him. Upon hearing that his fellow Christian worker had been arrested, Peter went to see if he could help Michael and was also arrested.

Peter recalls, "I was taken into a darkened cell. . . . The only contact I had with anyone was when food was passed to me through a very small opening in the door. . . . They would blindfold me to take me to interrogations. When the blindfold was removed, I would find four soldiers with guns pointing at me."

Michael was placed in a cell so crowded the inmates had to sleep in shifts. When he tells the story, he doesn't complain. On the contrary, he says this "was a perfect evangelism opportunity."

Both pastors were then transferred together to hot and crowded cells, where they had an opportunity to get Bibles and preach. Finally, they were relocated to death row for "offending Islamic beliefs." Since nothing more could be done to them, they lived up to the charges, leading other death row inmates to Christ.

"This was our mission field!" Peter said. "Michael and I worked out a schedule to preach with the permission of the prison officers who were very good to us."

They were again transferred. This time the guards let them have Bibles as long as they didn't preach.

Peter said, "It was the best place and the happiest phase for me because I was put in the same cell with condemned persons and had opportunity to preach to all. . . . We did not mind this because in this way we got access to almost all the condemned persons! God surely has His ways of doing things, even using those who think they are punishing you."

Peter and Michael were called into court a final time, knowing they would be either released or executed but feeling at peace with either outcome. They were living this biblical passage: "It is my eager expectation and hope that I will not be at all ashamed, but that with full courage now as always Christ will be honored in my body, whether by life or by death" (Philippians 1:20, ESV).

Both men were astonished when they were released!

After their long imprisonment, Peter said, "Through

our experiences condemned persons heard the gospel. . . . Also, . . . people around the world became aware of the pressures Christians face there. If our imprisonment was God's way of exposing their suffering so that they can receive relief and prayer support, it was worth it."

Pastor Michael pleads with Christians, "Please continue to pray for Sudan. Many are weak and remain weak under constant government pressure. They need training, prayer, and support. Pray for strength to all who are involved in church ministry."

Lord, I lift my voice with these two Christian heroes, asking you to strengthen their persecuted countrymen and Christians everywhere who suffer under Sharia law. You delivered these pastors from "deadly peril," and I ask you to deliver those who are imprisoned elsewhere. Yet, while they are there, make them lights of your Good News! Help me, Lord, to set my hope on you as they did. Help me to trust you more, so I, too, can see my struggles as blessings in disguise.

DAY 40

SELFLESSNESS IS SPIRITUAL LIBERATION

God is our refuge and strength, an ever-present help in trouble. Therefore we will not fear, though the earth give way and the mountains fall into the heart of the sea.

PSALM 46:1-2

EVEN IF OUR FAITH never costs us our lives, it has to cost us our *selves*. In the West, we work to extend our lives, to protect our lives, to improve our lives. But in the persecuted church, Christians do not think as much about self-preservation as they do about self-sacrifice. Consider this convert from Libya, the last place on earth anyone from the West would probably want to live.

"Maizah" was beaten, coerced to become a man's fourth wife, and threatened with death by her own family. What brought all that about? As a child, Maizah started questioning her religion. Once an imam beat her for wearing trousers, and when she attended a more liberal mosque, they accused her of "cheating God" because she didn't stay covered when not at worship. She caught her accusers lying and also "cheating God," so she left the mosque.

Years later, Maizah cried out for God in a darkened room. Suddenly a man shining like light touched her feet. He said, "I am the way, the truth, and the life." Two weeks later, war broke out and her family fled to Egypt as bombs fell.

In Egypt, a Christian neighbor befriended Maizah. Maizah asked her about Jesus. One day, she confided in the neighbor about the man she saw. The neighbor showed her John 14:6, the passage where Jesus said he was the way, the truth, and the life. Maizah converted to Christianity and returned to Libya, knowing she could be arrested or killed, just so she could be a light in the darkness.

Maizah joined a secret Libyan church when she arrived. Soon, Christians in the secret church were arrested, and people warned Maizah that the police were searching for her, too. She fled to Turkey, only to be told in a desperate telephone call with her sister to return to Egypt because their mother was sick.

When Maizah reunited with her family in Egypt, she discovered her mother was healthy; it was an attempt to entrap her for her faith. Her mother's house was filled with men who questioned Maizah and then beat her severely. One offered to take her as his fourth wife to keep her from being executed. She agreed but said she'd need to see a doctor. He didn't want her to go to a Libyan hospital. The man allowed her to go under guard to Tunisia, where the doctor she saw helped her escape to a safe house. Eventually, she made her way to the West, where she is still hiding from her family today.

Christian refugees like Maizah take seriously the psalmist who wrote, "The LORD is my rock, my fortress and my deliverer; my God is my rock, in whom I take refuge, my shield and the horn of my salvation, my stronghold" (Psalm 18:2). Although life is difficult for them, it is also simple: Jesus gave his life for them, so they are willing to give their lives for him, whether by death, imprisonment, exile, or the loss of everything they have ever known or loved.

For many of us in the West, we struggle to let go of our stuff. Let the simple, sacrificial faith of Maizah serve as a plumb line for you today, to see how far you may have drifted from the simplicity of living all in for Jesus. Christianity should cost us more than our 10 percent tithe and occasional church attendance. Let Jesus be Lord of *all* today, your refuge and strength, the ever-present help in your trouble.

As you finish this study, you might start it all over again or give a copy to a friend. Or maybe you'll never pick it up again. But, whatever you do, live a little more selflessly from this day forward. Let this day be a day that changes you for every day to come.

Selfishness is spiritual treason. Selflessness is spiritual *liberation*. Jesus gave everything for us; surely, we can give a little more for him. That alone will make you more like Jesus than almost anything else, and that alone will prepare you to live in solidarity with the suffering church like never before.

God, thank you for the example of persecuted believers who live selflessly for you. Please free me of selfishness and make me more selfless for you.

INTRODUCTION

I'LL NEVER FORGET witnessing two thousand followers of Jesus take a martyr's oath.

I was in India attending the graduation at a Bible school founded by one of my mentors, the late Bishop M. A. Thomas. He not only knew firsthand the sting of persecution and the reality of holding a minority faith in a dangerous world, but he also knew the power of God's love to soften even the hardest heart. Born into poverty, he had walked across India to the area where God called him, wearing a giant placard with the gospel written on it so he could minister along the way. Once he arrived, he was thrown in prison, but he led so many inmates to Christ that the jailers kicked them all out. Those inmates became the first members of his church.

The ministry he founded in Kota in 1960 grew and eventually established ninety-five Bible institutes, sixty-one orphanages, forty-three thousand church plants, a hospital, medical clinics, substance abuse programs, and a publishing arm that prints literature in the countless languages of India.[1] And as a bishop, he oversaw ten thousand churches, many of which were planted in leper colonies. He survived at least fifteen assassination attempts and walked with a limp because he was beaten so many times. Yet he wore a prominent cross around his neck to ensure extremists would recognize him. He was not ashamed of the cross.

Bishop Thomas made it clear that each of his students would be qualified for graduation only once they stood and confessed their willingness to serve Jesus even if it meant their death. They were to repeat after him, word for word, a martyr's oath. And they did—standing in an open-air tent next to a church that was too small to house them all. To this day, that church has a memorial next to its platform listing the names of the graduates who have already been martyred for Jesus.

One year extremists threw Molotov cocktails over the wall during a gathering the day before the graduation service, threatening to kill Bishop Thomas and burn the church. I can still hear Bishop Thomas's resonant voice booming over the microphone. "Listen to me!" he said. "Tomorrow there will be a service at this church. It will be a funeral service or a graduation service, but there will be a service!"

He was fearless.

The first time I witnessed the graduation, it shook my faith in a way I had never felt before. The temperatures soared over one hundred degrees without even a whiff of breeze, and an aroma of spices and humanity filled the still air as two thousand students pressed together with their family and friends. Unlike the American culture I was accustomed to, no one complained about the heat, the smell, or the inconvenience while singing "I Surrender All."

Word by word, the resolute roar of the students' voices rose from that dusty tent as they pledged their lives and deaths to Jesus. I remember thinking that I was standing in the book of Acts, witnessing a raw, first-century Christianity that I'd been shielded from in the United States. I felt deprived yet suddenly spiritually alive in an entirely new way.

My faith finally made sense. All the disparate parts of the New Testament came together in my heart as I witnessed this authentic expression of faith in Jesus. *Real* faith in Jesus. These bold brothers and sisters weren't just willing to live for Jesus; they were willing to die for him.

I asked myself—as I have a thousand times since—*Why*

are so few of us in America willing to live for Jesus when others are so willing to die for him? Seeing Jesus through the eyes of the persecuted church transformed me.

I've written this book because I believe seeing your faith through their eyes will change you, too. My prayer for you is that their stories will change your life in a way you desperately need. Perhaps it will change you in a way you don't even know you need.

I've also written this book because the Bible declares, "If one part [of the body] suffers, all the parts suffer with it" (1 Corinthians 12:26, NLT). I feel like we barely care or barely know the stories of our persecuted brothers and sisters. Either is an unspeakable tragedy. As my friends at Open Doors International are fond of saying, "If you follow Jesus, there's a part of your family you need to know: those who are suffering and those who will die for Jesus."

Some estimate that every five minutes, a Christian is martyred for the faith.[2] For many, avoiding martyrdom is as simple as writing or even saying that they renounce their faith in Jesus. For these martyred believers, the gospel is so precious, the comfort of the Holy Spirit so tangible, and the example of those Christians who have come before them so compelling that they will not weaken or renounce their faith—regardless of the cost.

It has cost them their lives. The gospel has cost most of us nothing.

My team and I have crisscrossed the world, recorders in hand, to gather reports from survivors, asking them to tell us what God is doing in and through ordinary people who meet extraordinary circumstances with overcoming faith.

In these pages, I relate what they said, using their exact words. We've transcribed their stories, connecting each with observations about the suffering they face and the lessons to be learned. In every story, as in the declarations of those graduates from Bishop Thomas's school, you will find a willingness to live and to die for Christ.

Like the family we met in the Middle East who found faith in Christ as refugees fleeing the Syrian war. They were jihadists themselves until they encountered Jesus in a miraculous way. The news made it all the way back to one of their adult siblings in Syria, prompting a strongly worded message in reply, guaranteeing their death by crucifixion if they did not return to Islam. The new follower of Jesus replied to his brother-in-law, "We are willing to die for Jesus, but please do not crucify us. We are not worthy of dying in the same way as our Savior."

Unlike the jihadist martyrs gaining the attention—and fear—of the world, these followers of Jesus are not seeking to die in order to *earn* a place in heaven. They are willing to die as an expression of gratitude for *having already received* the gift of God's salvation through Jesus and his promise to live together in a real, eternal heaven. They die with prayers of love and forgiveness on their lips. In their dying breaths, they profess Jesus' kindness and love for the world.

And that's another reason I've written this book. In a time when we are witnessing martyrdom and persecution akin to that endured by our brothers and sisters in the first century, we are also seeing the same miraculous works as those days in the early church. Nearly every day, a terrorist is encountering Jesus on a road to Damascus. There are countless "apostle Pauls" emerging in our time. Many of them are converted as miraculously as he was, and many of them will suffer and die as he did. All of them believe that Jesus is the only real hope in the world.

First-century persecution in the twenty-first century—while horrific and evil—is also producing a first-century harvest of millions coming to follow Jesus in the most miraculous ways and from the most unlikely places.

Here are their true stories, and my hope is that by the end of this book, you, too, will be willing to take the Martyr's Oath, which I have included at both the beginning and the end of this book. The title of each chapter is taken from the oath, and the stories within each chapter illustrate what it means to live out this statement.

If you are ready to stand with Christians around the world in harm's way and take the Martyr's Oath, then go to www.MartyrsOath.com and take your stand.

More important, I hope you learn how to live for the Jesus they are willing to die for, wherever you are and whether it costs you anything—or everything.

Johnnie Moore
The Netherlands
2016

CHAPTER 1

I AM A FOLLOWER OF JESUS

We are hard-pressed on every side, yet not crushed; we are perplexed, but not in despair; persecuted, but not forsaken; struck down, but not destroyed.

2 CORINTHIANS 4:8-9, NKJV

MORE CHRISTIANS were martyred for their faith in the twentieth century than in all previous centuries combined.[1]

Some people are fond of saying that the persecution Christians are now facing is just history repeating itself. They suggest it's the same as it has ever been, but that is not the case. Persecution against Christians has dramatically escalated, and the scale of the brutality has worsened.

Open Doors International, an organization that ranks levels of persecution around the world, has noted that, conservatively, more than 7,100 Christians were killed for their faith in 2015. That's nearly double the number killed in 2014 and more than triple the number killed in 2013.[2] The actual number is probably much higher. Statistics are hard to come by in countries that behead, burn alive, and enslave people.

It's as if Satan himself is playing for keeps, employing astonishing efforts to wipe the followers of Jesus from the face of the earth—to finish us off and to do it with all the spectacle he possibly can. Yet Christianity is now the largest religion in the world, with more than two billion believers worldwide.[3]

What is it about Christianity that has caused so much hate to be unleashed against it?

It comes down to what we believe, which I've summarized in the Martyr's Oath:

> I am a follower of Jesus. I believe he lived and walked among us, was crucified for our sins, and was raised from the dead, according to the Scriptures. I believe he is the King of the earth, who will come back for his church.

In his day, the apostle Paul wrote that "the message of the cross is foolishness to those who are perishing"

(1 Corinthians 1:18). And we see that same opinion shared today, especially as Christian faith is pushed out of the public arena in secular states. But in some parts of the world, believing in Christ is seen as worse than foolishness. It's viewed as a threat, and it comes with a death sentence.

Under Communist regimes, where the state demands full and unquestioning loyalty, Christians' beliefs that Jesus is Lord and that our citizenship is in heaven are viewed as seditious. And in the Islamic world, believing that Jesus is the only way to God the Father is viewed as blasphemy.

As we consider at the outset of the book what it means to be followers of Jesus, I want you to read these stories from Christians in Nigeria, in their own words. In Nigeria, simply following Jesus has cost some faithful believers nearly everything.

DORIS, UCHE, AND GABRIEL || *Nigeria*

Christmas Eve 2010 in Jos, Nigeria: the streets are buzzing with last-minute shoppers in a crowded suburb. Doris, a widow of just one year, browses the shops. The mother of five needs just one more item to start her cooking.

Middle-aged Uche, sporting short-cropped hair and a

mustache, is walking from work to the market to buy supplies for his family's Christmas celebration.

Gabriel is a father of two, with a slender build and wearing a thin, short-sleeved white oxford shirt with no pocket. He tends his mother's fabric shop and notices something is off. He has come to this part of town just to help her after taking time off from his own work. While busying himself, he sees a few men drop off a package at the shop. He thinks it's strange, but like other shop owners and shoppers, he doesn't do anything about it—it's Christmas Eve, and everyone just wants to get home to their families.

As the clock ticks toward 7:00 p.m., a series of blasts shakes the market. A transit bus bursts into flames, streaking the night sky with orange and red. Burning shops, homes, and automobiles add an eerie, dancing light. Building walls are sprayed with black film. The smell of chemicals, heat, and charred wood permeates the air. The streets are littered with food, clothes, and body parts.

Doris, Uche, and Gabriel are just a few of the hundreds who have faced constant hardships since the blasts. Yet they are lucky. Nearby, two churches were attacked, and another bombing targeted a Christian area. In all, more than eighty funerals were held in the few days following the attack.

Yet the church remains, and the survivors choose to remain. They continue to speak Jesus' name and to tell of his grace with boldness. Silence would mean security. Fleeing would mean safety. But it isn't about security and safety to them. It's about the privilege to be the light of Jesus in the very darkest places.

DORIS

"I was in the market, and I was on my way back when a bomb went off near a bridge. I had stopped to buy spices so I could cook. The bomb went off, and I was lifted off the ground. When I fell down, I tried to stand up. But I fell down again, and I realized my leg had been blown off.

After the accident, I was taken to the hospital, and my leg had to be amputated. Now I walk slowly. I fall down. I don't even know who paid for my medical bills. It might have been the government, but I don't know for sure.

My church has been helpful. I have five children, and they support me as well. I live with my daughter and her husband. I am following the Lord strongly because he spared me. Many died that day, so I have a lot that I owe him. I always thank him. Since he spared me, it means he wants me to carry on his work. ”

UCHE

“God has blessed me with three children. I am a metalworker, and on Christmas Eve, I got off work early for the celebration. I went to the market very close to where I live to buy things for our Christmas celebration. I heard the sound of a bomb nearby, and when it went off, I lost both of my legs.

They took me to the hospital, and from there I spent months in the hospital. My colleagues helped pay my medical bills. I finished the treatments and then went back home with two artificial legs. I still have expensive medicines I have to buy. My wife would not stay. She left me and the children.

I can't go back to my job, so it is hard to pay school fees for my children. We struggle to pay for where we live, but we cannot afford to move. Life isn't easy for our family.

From the beginning, I gave my life to God. I know he will never leave me. Whatever the reason for why this happened to me, I know he will meet my needs."

GABRIEL

"I am a worker and have two children. My mom has her own fabric shop in a market.

On Christmas Eve, I took off work to help her at her shop because she had lots of customers coming. I noticed Muslims came and left something nearby. But I didn't pay attention, because I was busy. Around 7:00 p.m., the bomb blew up in the shop.

It killed many people. That's how I got this injury on my leg. I was rushed to a nearby hospital, where they started treatment. There were not enough doctors to treat me. I had my leg amputated and now have an artificial limb.

Now, I've been buying medicine day in and day out. I cannot work at my old job. My mother is aging. Her business has collapsed. She is depressed. I can't work enough, and I can't care for her. My children are still small. They look up to me. But I cannot even pick them up because I can't lift heavy things now. My injuries handicap me.

My mother depends on me. She needs me to help care for her financially. But I depend on others to give me simple jobs. I have to care for my wife and children, too, so I need consistent work.

I'm telling you, this is real life for us. It's only through the help of God that we have survived.

We all believe in Christ. He is our personal Lord and Savior, and with him all things are possible. He is our source. Man cannot give you these things, so I stand strongly in my faith. Without him we can do nothing.”

HANNAH || *Nigeria*

Sixteen-year-old Abigail was asleep in her school's dormitory during finals week. Only one assignment stood between her and the close of the school year. She would soon be home and enjoying the life of a teenage girl.

As she slept, Abigail didn't know of the phone calls coming to her area from neighboring villages, warning that the terrorist group Boko Haram was on the way. She didn't know of the failed attempts to get more security to her school. She probably didn't even know that Boko Haram had threatened to burn schools and kidnap children. All she knew was that she was surrounded by her friends and classmates, her parents lived nearby, security forces were outside her dorm, and she had just one more assignment to finish.

Today, Abigail has been featured in a Boko Haram video released to prove that the 276 schoolgirls kidnapped on the night of April 14, 2014, are still alive. Obviously under duress, she states in her native Hausa language, "Our parents should take heart. Talk to the government so that we can be allowed to go home. Please come to our rescue. The aircraft have come and killed many of us. We are really suffering here. There is no food to eat, no good water to drink."

A terrorist then takes to the screen to repeat their same demands, that the government release imprisoned Boko Haram fighters. "Or we will never release these girls."

Reports of the kidnapped girls electrified the media within thirty-six hours of the assault on their school. The kidnapping arrested the attention of the entire world, with millions tweeting #BringBackOurGirls. Even former US First Lady Michelle Obama joined in the social-media advocacy. Yet all civilian and government efforts couldn't convince Boko Haram of the evil they'd done. They kept the girls, forcibly converted them to Islam, and made some of them sexual slaves and others soldiers.

Today, a "BBOG" Facebook page features scores of likes.[4] *An outspoken BBOG activist group helped elect a new Nigerian president whose campaign promises included finding the girls. With that hope dashed, the BBOG campaign continues staging protests and rallies to keep the vanished girls before the eyes of the world.*

Hannah, Abigail's mother, has been in the news herself, criticizing the government for not rescuing the girls and blaming it on the fact that her village is poor.

Around 135 of the original girls have now escaped or been released. But not Abigail. She's still lost.

Hannah wears a head wrapper made of a bright geometric print that matches her dress. She holds her head upright and speaks in declarative statements tinged with defiance. She talks freely until she comes to the end of her story. Then she speaks wistfully, with long pauses. And then she weeps. She just weeps. She is grateful to God for the four children she has, yet nothing takes the place of her baby.

She is spirited. She is passionate. She is a mother. She is determined. She is hopeful. She is angry.[5]

> "It was an awful night, April 14, 2014. We had no information, no idea, no news, nothing. We just heard gunshots coming from the direction of her boarding school. *Lord, my daughter!* All my knowledge, my brain, my head, my strength, my energy went out to that school.

We had heard they planned to attack schools and kidnap kids. I called my sister. She didn't know anything. She said, "Just give up for the night." But I said, "I [am] going to the school for my baby!"

My husband stopped me. He said, "There is security in the school." But I could hear the gunshots, so I planned to go fight. I grabbed some rocks because we have rocks everywhere.

It was the long, long night.

There were normally fourteen or fifteen security soldiers. But they could not win. We don't know what happened. But we heard Boko Haram from 11:00 p.m. until 4:00 in the morning—shooting, burning. At 4:00 a.m. it became quiet, so we rushed to the school. The girls were gone. We saw their uniforms, their dresses, everything scattered everywhere. We thought the girls had tried to escape or the security had rescued them or something of that nature. But the whole school was burned. They destroyed the roof. They burned out everything.

We met one girl, and I asked her, "Where are the girls?" She said, "I don't know." I kept crying,

"Where is my baby?" I called her name, "Abigail!" The girl said, "Maybe she went home." She didn't know what happened. I screamed, "She is not at home!" Then I asked her more questions. The girl said that night she was not feeling well. She was sleeping in some other dormitory when the noise from Boko Haram woke her up as they burned the building. Before she came out, she realized the heat of the fire was too much, so she climbed out the window and onto a tree. She climbed down, then climbed over a fence and ran away. That's how she escaped.

We talked to her and then stayed at the school, hoping to see our girls. After an hour or two, some girls came walking toward the school. We rushed to them and said, "What's happened?" They said, "Boko Haram has kidnapped and packed up all of them."

"How did they pack them up?" I asked. They said, "In a truck." The escaped girls said they packed them in trucks and cars and carted them away.

It was a government-run "comprehensive

boarding school," so the boys went in the morning for the lectures. In the evening, after closing hours, the boys would go home. But the girls stayed in the dormitory. So the boys were secured because they were home with their parents. But the girls . . . the girls . . . that happened to them!

I talked to many girls. Many girls. I tried to sort out where my baby was. I have a cousin who was with her, who escaped. She said Abigail was in the truck close to the driver. Abigail couldn't jump out. My cousin called to her that she was dropping out of the truck, but Abigail just couldn't make it. She couldn't escape.

Another girl, before she escaped the next day, said she saw my baby sleeping. Abigail was tired because as they were driving, their truck broke down. So they had to trek on foot to the Sambisa Forest. That's where they are to this day.

Now there is a negotiator with Boko Haram, and they got fifteen of the girls and interviewed them on December 25 last year. They still have hundreds of girls in captivity. The military is combing the forest, still looking for them. They say the place is too dangerous. They can't enter with firepower because that could harm the girls. Maybe Boko Haram will harm the girls. Maybe Boko Haram will use the girls as a human shield.

My baby was not yet sixteen, but now she is eighteen. She was writing her final paper. I don't know where she might be. I am hoping that one day we will see them. Prayer is the only key to success. With God, it is possible. He is a great God. My baby . . . ”

Make no mistake. Both the Jos market bombing and Boko Haram's kidnapping of schoolgirls targeted the victims because of their Christianity. The extremists have gone from one Christian village to the next, terrorizing Nigeria's Christians. In one province alone, more than 70 percent of the churches have been destroyed.

Jesus tells his disciples, "If you do not carry your own cross and follow me, you cannot be my disciple. But don't begin until you count the cost" (Luke 14:27-28, NLT). For many Christians around the world, and for those who tell their stories here, they have counted the cost. Whatever they suffer, whether they give up their health, their livelihoods, or even their lives, they recognize that Jesus is greater than it all.

I wonder how many of us in the United States have counted the cost of following Jesus—I mean *really* counted the cost. For some of us, we may think we have. We just don't think we need Jesus very much. Jesus is the ultimate "value add" to whatever version of the good life we've fashioned, the capstone to a life well lived. He gives unilateral approval to our decisions and may get us out of a jam now and then, but he doesn't require much from us. We don't demand much of him, so he can't demand much of us.

I want to draw your attention to Gabriel's brave words: "We all believe in Christ. He is our personal Lord and Savior, and with him all things are possible. He is our source. Man cannot give you these things, so I stand strongly in my faith. Without him we can do nothing."

Without him we can do nothing.

In our self-reliant, individualistic culture, these words are radical. They are an acknowledgment of Jesus' lordship, his authority over every area of our lives. And Jesus' authority is one that we willingly, lovingly, and eagerly must submit to.

What does it mean for those of us who are in the most prosperous nation on earth to join with those who are losing their lives for believing in Jesus? What does counting the cost look like for us?

These brave believers who are so confident and fearless in their testimony, even in the face of horrific loss, show us the way. For sure, believers around the world need our prayers, and they need our financial support. It's not unusual for social support systems to be nonexistent for Christians in countries where Christian persecution is common. And those Christians who manage to escape are often not allowed to work in the countries that have granted them refuge, leaving them in jeopardy. They need *our* help.[6]

But we also need *their* help.

For all that we may be doing to help them, they also help us. They inspire us to a deeper place in our commitment to Jesus. They inspire us to *live* for the Jesus they are willing to *die* for. Their testimonies call us to take our own faith more seriously, and they lead us to discover the true power of Jesus.

NOTES

INTRODUCTION

1. The ministry continues today under the leadership of his amazing son, Samuel Thomas. See *Hopegivers*, www.hopegivers.org.
2. Michael F. Haverluck, "Every 5 Minutes, a Christian Is Martyred," *One News Now*, September 20, 2015, http://www.onenewsnow.com/persecution/2015/09/20/every-5-minutes-a-christian-is-martyred.

CHAPTER 1: I Am a Follower of Jesus

1. George Weigel, "Rediscovering the Martyrology," *First Things*, February 26, 2014, https://www.firstthings.com/web-exclusives/2014/02/rediscovering-the-martyrology.
2. Stephen Rand, "Freedom of Religion and the Persecution of Christians: The Open Doors Report, 2016," Open Doors, https://www.opendoorsuk.org/persecution/documents/ww-report-160113.pdf.
3. Bill Chappell, "World's Muslim Population Will Surpass Christians This Century, Pew Says," *The Two-Way*, April 2, 2015, http://www.npr.org/sections/thetwo-way/2015/04/02/397042004/muslim-population-will-surpass-christians-this-century-pew-says.
4. Bring Back Our Girls' Facebook page, accessed March 22, 2017, https://www.facebook.com/bringbackourgirls/.
5. Report drawn from live interview; Aminu Abubakar, "As Many as 200 Girls Abducted by Boko Haram, Nigerian Officials Say," CNN, April 16, 2014, http://www.cnn.com/2014/04/15/world/africa

/nigeria-girls-abducted/; Aminu Abubakar, Faith Karimi, and Michael Pearson, "Scared but Alive: Video Purports to Show Abducted Nigerian Girls," CNN, May 13, 2014, http://www.cnn.com/2014/05/12/world/africa/nigeria-abducted-girls/; and David Blair, "Boko Haram Releases New Video Claiming to Show Nigeria's Abducted Chibok Schoolgirls," *Telegraph*, August 14, 2016, http://www.telegraph.co.uk/news/2016/08/14/boko-haram-releases-new-video-of-alleged-chibok-girls/.

6. There are many great organizations you can give to in order to help them. You can contribute to World Help (www.worldhelp.net), Open Doors (www.opendoorsusa.org), or our own emergency relief fund, The KAIROS Trust (www.TheKAIROSTrust.com).

ABOUT THE AUTHOR

JOHNNIE MOORE, author of the highly acclaimed *Defying ISIS*, is a speaker and a humanitarian who has been called one of the "world's most influential young leaders" and "a modern-day Dietrich Bonhoeffer." His advocacy has provided tens of millions of dollars in emergency assistance to persecuted Christians, and in 2015 he helped lead the charge to get genocide resolutions against ISIS passed unanimously in both houses of the United States Congress and in the British and European parliaments. He is a member of the White House Faith Advisory Council and is a recipient of the prestigious medal of valor from the Simon Wiesenthal Center. Moore is also a widely read opinion columnist, having written for the *Washington Post*, Fox News, *Relevant* magazine, and CNN. He is a visiting lecturer at the Liberty University Center for Apologetics and Cultural Engagement, a fellow of the Townsend Institute for Leadership and Counseling at Concordia University, and an international spokesperson for the Museum of the Bible. He serves on the boards of the National Association of Evangelicals, the World Evangelical Alliance, World Help, the Dream Center LA, the Anti-Defamation League of Los Angeles, and My Faith Votes. He is the founder of The KAIROS Company.